MUST THE YOUNG DIE TOO?

WYATT SAWYER

GOSPEL ADVOCATE
A TRUSTED NAME SINCE 1855

Gospel Advocate Company
P.O. Box 150
Nashville, Tennessee 37202

Must the Young Die Too?
Gospel Advocate Reprint Library Edition, 2001

© 1955, Wyatt Sawyer

Published by Gospel Advocate Co.
P.O. Box 150, Nashville, TN 37202
www.gospeladvocate.com

ISBN: 0-89225-523-4

Preface

M UST THE YOUNG DIE TOO? was written
with two reading audiences in mind.
The first, an audience of young people; and
the second, their parents.

This story is based on true experiences
and a true life character. To protect those
who were involved all names have been
changed, as well as some places and events.

It is the author's earnest hope and prayer
that everyone who reads this book will be
awakened to the serious problems which
face our young people in the rapidly changing American culture. A sympathetic understanding is of utmost importance.

It is believed that within the pages of
this volume lies the only real solution to our
ever-increasing juvenile delinquency and
adult moral decline.

Introduction

A HOPELESS ETERNITY is rapidly taking our young people all too soon! It is later than we think! Our dangerous age demands action at once!

After reading *Must the Young Die Too?* by Wyatt Sawyer, it is my firm conviction that it will be a book to serve and bless humanity at a time when most needed. It is going to help us turn to God and His Word in a time of moral crisis! This book is unique and different from any other in its field.

The author has had wide experience in youth work and parental relations. He is amply qualified in education, personal effort and unfeigned love for suffering souls to make the right approach at the right time. This he very aptly does in *Must the Young Die Too?*

The world is now waiting anxiously for a solution to its grave moral and social problems. *Back to the Bible is the only recourse. Must the Young Die Too?* will rapidly take the lead in this drastic situation when once released from the press.

Our present atom-hydrogen age rocks the world in fear, because of immoral and modernistic control of things. The passing of one more generation of our children without a turn to the right way of life could wreck all civilization. But just one generation of well trained young people in righteousness will save the day! *Must the Young Die Too?* is coming to the rescue! A copy of this book should be studied by the parents and young people of every home.

Must the Young Die Too? reaches the human heart from every angle of human nature. It strikes at the very roots of crime and pulls those roots up for exposure. It puts God and the church first and draws upon the Bible for its power! Every stage of life, from the cradle to the grave, is well pictured in terms that reach the heart. The gospel plan of salvation is skilfully woven into the sequence of the book in a way to be accepted. This book is going to live! The warmth, zeal, logic, and gentle admonition and appeal melt the heart to tears!

Must the Young Die Too? will serve a two-fold purpose. First, it will fire the members of the Lord's church with new zeal, knowledge and determination. Second, it will reach thousands of souls lost in the darkness of moral shame and cold indifference.

This book should be bought for young and old alike. It should be used in study courses, given as wedding presents, birthday and holiday gifts. This book has my full indorsement.

JAMES L. NEAL
Editor, *The Gospel Age*

Springdale, Arkansas

Acknowledgment

I WISH to express my sincerest appreciation to the many friends who read this volume before its publication and who made invaluable suggestions.

I am especially indebted to Mrs. Johnny Braddy of Fort Worth, Texas for her reviews of the manuscript in that city before public audiences to test its public appeal and apparent worth.

THE AUTHOR

Dedication

To my devoted wife, Christine, and our two sons, Jerry Kent and Joel Grant.

Table of Contents

CHAPTER 1
ROGER SCOTT—YOUNG CRIMINAL

"My name is Roger Scott. I am a murderer! However, I don't look like one at all. I stand 5' 10" tall. I have brownish-red hair and brown eyes. I weigh 155 pounds. They tell me I look like any other average American young man. I am twenty-six years old."

"I've been in the courtroom now nearly an hour waiting for my trial to begin. I'm very nervous. I'll be glad to get this over with because I've been dreading this ordeal for about a year. Some have told me I should be acquitted. Others are doing everything in their power to put me in the electric chair. The Judge is coming in now."

The Judge is a very large judicious-looking man with a booming voice equal to his stature. His first words rebounded off the back wall and stopped the low muttering of the overflow crowd of curious people, thrill-seekers and town gossips.

"In this case a young man must stand trial before a jury of his peers," began the Judge. "I think I need not remind those present that this is a most grave occasion. The outcome of these proceedings will determine whether this young man will live or must die for his crime."

"I gripped my chair hard when the Judge said those last words. I still hadn't gotten used to the idea that I might die before I'm thirty. I was scared—plenty scared. My quivering lips were only a slight evidence of my real inward agony and fear. I had rehearsed this moment a thousand times in my cell. It was easy to be calm and sophisticated there. But here it's different. There are hundreds of people here; some are for me and some are against me. Some of them hope I die."

A low murmur rumbled through the courtroom as the overflow crowd reacted in shock to the thought that this fine looking young man might soon die.

"I must remind you men of the jury that you bear a solemn obligation to the State. You also owe this young man a fair and impartial hearing. The purpose of this court is that justice may be done. Therefore, I charge you individually to weigh all the facts carefully and come to an honest verdict."

"The court is now ready for trial," said the Judge as he turned his attention from the jury to the lawyers seated before him. "Is the State ready with its case?"

"We are ready, your Honor," replied the State's attorney.

"Is the Defense ready?" the Judge continued.

"The Defense is ready for trial," replied one of Roger's court-appointed lawyers.

"Then let us proceed with the case. The State will now present its evidence."

One of the State's attorneys arose and faced the jury. "The defendant, Roger Scott, is being charged with murder in the first degree. His signed confession which I hold as exhibit "A" admits that he brutally slaughtered three men on a lonely State road early one morning. We have no alternative in the face of the facts but to demand the death penalty for this man. After all, this was cold-blooded homicide. We would like our first witness, a Mr. Simmons to come to the stand."

Kindly old Mr. Simmons took the stand and after being given the oath to tell the truth he sat down in the witness chair.

Roger listened to Mr. Simmon's testimony attentively for awhile. Then his mind wandered back to that fateful night when he fought with the three men, he later killed and . . . . but his thoughts were rudely interrupted when the lawyer shook an old revolver in his face.

"This is the gun he used to kill those men last December a year ago, isn't it Mr. Simmons?" And forgetting himself for a moment in the passion of his charges the lawyer turned accusingly to Roger. "This is the gun you killed Benjamin Peebles, Arthur Miles and Jim Southy with isn't it, Mr. Scott, alias Ben Brown?"

Both of Roger's lawyers were on their feet shaking their fists toward the Judge's bench. "We object, your Honor," said one,

"Our client is not on the witness stand. This questioning is most irregular!"

"Objection sustained!" replied the Judge as he pounded his gavel. "The State's attorney is asked to confine his questions to the witness on the stand."

The lawyer gave a rather sheepish nod toward the Judge and resumed his questioning of Mr. Simmons.

"Alright, sir, is this the revolver the defendant gave you the morning he was captured?"

"Well now, I don't know. That sorta looks like the gun."

"My dear sir, this is a court of law. We must have positive facts. Be specific sir! Is this the gun he gave you to turn in to the police?"

"Just can't tell you for sure, young man," replied the farmer, "I ain't got my specks on me and I can't be specific about nothing, less I have 'em."

"And where are your glasses, sir?" asked the impatient attorney.

"Mama's got them in her purse right over there."

"Then by all means let's get Mama to part with them long enough for you to identify this gun."

The court proceedings came to a standstill while Mama Simmons pillaged through the contents of her bulky purse. Presently she located the glasses and handed them to the waiting lawyer.

"Now that you can see better, will you positively state that this is the gun which was given you by the defendant?"

"Yes sir, that's it! Don't believe I could mistake it at all. It had a chip out of the handle on the right side. Let's see. There it is. That's the gun alright."

"I watched the lawyer take the gun from Mr. Simmons and put it back on the table across from me. It brought back bitter memories."

•

"The whole incident was still vivid in my mind. I could never forget that night. There were those three drunks and we had a fight and I shot them. I can still hear the echos as they traveled through the swamp and down into the bayou. And the men? I remember them too. My .38 was talking to *them* in a language they could understand. I hadn't expected to ever use the gun, I just had it along in case. Now I wish I'd left it where it belonged."

"I've asked myself thousands of times why I did such a thing. But I still don't know. One thing led to another, then it was all over before I realized what happened. It was too late to think then."

The lawyer continued to cross-question Mr. Simmons. He was determined to establish a case against Roger which would be beyond a reasonable doubt in the jury's mind. The State knew it had a strong case and it pressed every advantage.

"I kept telling myself this didn't make sense. I didn't mean to get into any trouble. I was just walking down that highway that morning in the cold rain. I was tired and sick and hungry. It must have been about 1:30 because we left that filling station at one and we had driven at least thirty minutes. Those men were drinking heavily and they got a real kick out of trying to get me to drink with them. I think they started out to make a joke of it, but they didn't stop there. There were three of them and they knew they could make me do almost anything if they wanted to, so they tried. I got really scared when they pulled over to the side of the road and pulled me out of the car. They got awfully unreasonable after that. I didn't know what to do. I tried to run once, but my legs were so swollen and sore I didn't get very far before they caught me. This made them angry I guess because they shoved me down and one of them began to kick me. They ruffled me up good after that and I was taking it pretty good until one of them kicked me in the head. That made me see stars and I got real mad. That was the last straw and I was determined not to take any more. People had pushed me around all my life and I decided this was one time I was going to push back. I had never hurt anyone before, but neither had they ever hurt me this bad either. So as soon as I got my hand free I jerked out my revolver and started firing. They sounded mighty surprised when they started feeling my lead. But they left me alone after that. Then I don't remember what happened.

I guess I was too numb or stunned or something. The police said I took all their wallets, but I don't remember doing that."

After the shooting Roger did search the dead men's pockets and take their valuables. Then without looking in any direction he began to hobble away from the bloody scene. He ran into the swamp-lands and kept moving until he was several miles away. When he felt that he was at a safe distance he sat down on a tree stump to get his breath.

●

"Large beads of sweat came on my forehead as I sat there thinking about my awful crime again. One of my lawyers noticed me and whispered to me."

"What's the matter son? Are you living it all over again?"

I nodded my head and whispered back to him. "I'm not sure whether its that or my fever. I surely don't feel very well."

The State's attorney finished his questioning of Mr. Simmons and called for other witnesses. At this point the case against Roger was looking very bad. The way the State was guiding the evidence, the audience would think he had never had a good thought in his life. But the true facts alone testified that he was a thief and a murderer.

"This whole trial seemed very needless to me. I had signed a confession stating my guilt to all these things. I told everybody I was guilty so I didn't see any use in them making me go through it all again. I told my lawyer how I felt too."

"You must understand Roger that this is the way we do things in this country. Trial by jury is one of our basic rights and is provided in the Constitution. Every man must go through a trial no matter how many confessions he signs. Some men have signed false confessions under duress you know and the trial later proved them innocent. Now try to be more patient. I know this is hard on you, but it will be the last time you have to go through it."

As the questioning continued it became apparent that there was little hope that Roger might be acquitted. Few, if any, had supposed that there would be. However, his lawyers were hoping to get him off with a life-imprisonment sentence at the most.

Earlier they had filed a plea of temporary insanity for him, but he had been judged sane at the lunacy hearing. So more and more Roger's attorneys knew they must plead self-defense and cast their defendant on the mercy of the jury.

"My lawyer said they had agreed not to call Mrs. Simmons to the witness stand, but they must have changed their minds. It was clear now that they weren't taking any chances. One of the State's men was a new lawyer who was recently admitted to the bar and he was determined to get a conviction in his first big case. The State knew that Mrs. Simmon's testimony could hurt Roger's chances of leniency so they called her as a surprise witness."

"Your name is Sarah Simmons?" the lawyer began.

"Yes sir," she replied in a soft voice.

"And the defendant ate supper with you and your husband about a year ago at your place?"

"That's right." she replied.

"Now in your own words tell this jury some of the details of this young man's visit in your home. And also tell them something of his conduct while there, if you please."

"Well sir, there isn't much to tell. He just came to our place and asked if we had any work he could do for his board and room for a few days. We have a small farm you know, so there wasn't anything we needed done, but we felt sorry for him and had him split some kindling for dad. He was dirty and his clothes were torn and we could tell he was sick and hadn't eaten much for several days. We didn't think he could harm anybody in his condition. He had such a kind face and Dad and me think those killings were just a big mistake anyway. We liked the boy."

"Pardon me for butting in this way Mrs. Simmons, but we would like you to refrain from giving any of your opinions about the defendant. Just tell us what happened. All we want is the facts."

"I object your honor!" exclaimed Roger's lawyer. "The lady was only doing what she was told to do. She was telling what happened and this jury has the right to know how they felt about my client. We therefore request that she be allowed to continue freely and without further interference."

"Objection overruled! The gentleman of the State asked for the facts, not personal opinion. Please, Mrs. Simmons, confine your remarks to the events that took place at your home."

"I'm very sorry, your Honor, I didn't mean to start a fuss between these nice gentlemen. I'll try to be more careful, but we did think a lot of that boy."

Mama Simmons then told how she and Mr. Simmons had taken a liking to Roger because he resembled their son who had been killed in the first World War.

"You say he looked a lot like your son? But in spite of that, were you ever afraid of him for any reason? Did his conduct there ever frighten you or make you think he might harm you in any way?"

"Land sakes no! There wasn't anything to be afraid of. He was a very sick boy. Why he was as gentle as my lap-cat, Catherine. No sir we weren't afraid of him for a minute."

"Well then, let's put it this way. Did you suspect him as being a killer?"

"No we didn't, did we dad?" she said appealing to her husband to reinforce her answer. Mr. Simmons rose from his seat and answered his wife. "No we didn't Mama."

The State's attorney turned to the Judge in haste. "Your Honor, may we ask that his lady refrain from violating the ethics of this court so grossly? This talking to her husband while under oath is most irregular!"

Underneath his poker-face the Judge grinned broadly. He was aware that Mama Simmons had never been in court before and was ignorant of the technicalities of jurisprudence. Nevertheless, he sustained the objection.

"Was Mr. Scott entirely normal in his conduct while at your house?" The lawyer continued. "You see it has been charged that this man was temporarily out of his mind the night before. Did you have any reason to believe that he was insane?"

"No sir, he wasn't insane at our place. He was very nervous, but his mind was good."

"Then you would say that he was rational all the time he was in your home, would you?"

"Yes, I guess so. He was a little strange at first, but we could tell he was a sick boy and we didn't pay that much mind. But he didn't act crazy or anything like that. As a matter of fact he was about the sanest person I ever knew. He did a wonderful thing that night."

"That's all, Mrs. Simmons. Step down please."

"But can't I tell you what a fine thing he did at our house?"

"Step down, please." the lawyer said in a firm tone.

Mama Simmons forgot that she was a witness for the State at this time. Since no one had said anything good about Roger until now she felt obligated to come to his defense. But the lawyer prevented her doing so.

●

"How well I remember the afternoon I stumbled onto the Simmon's place. I had fought my way through the swamps until daylight and I was hungry and exhausted. I hid out in the brush and slept until afternoon. Then I went up to the house and asked for food. I didn't know then that I had been traveling in circles much of the time and was only a few miles from the scene of the killings. I knocked at the Simmon's door and offered to work for a few days of board and room. The Simmons talked it over and invited me in. Supper was already on the table, all except the stew and it was nearly done. So I went out in the orchard and chopped some wood and then washed up for supper. The water from the well was cool and refreshing to my fevered skin so I let the bucket down again and poured a second bucket full of cool water down my arms and on the back of my neck."

"Inside the house a few minutes later I ate several large helpings of Mama Simmon's delicious Irish stew. At the table I introduced myself as Ben Brown during our conversation. I told them I was on my way home from a job in California. They noticed that my clothes looked rather strange, but they didn't ask too many questions."

A car drove up the lane and into the Simmon's yard as Roger was finishing a bowl of home-canned peaches. He was apprehensive at first and started to run out the back door, but Mrs. Simmons calmed his fears.

"Look dad, that's Emma and the children. How nice that they should come over this evening. What's the matter Ben? Don't be alarmed, its just a neighbor of ours and her children. They come to see us every day or two."

"I was afraid the car was the police coming after me, but I settled down when I heard the woman's voice and the children's. Mrs. Simmons introduced me to Mrs. Miles and her three children, Dorothy, Marie and Billy. She was very upset I could tell. Her eyes were red and she looked as if she had been crying a long time. When I saw her great distress I excused myself and crawled into the attic room where the Simmons told me I could sleep."

Once comfortable in the feather mattress Roger began to think. Hardly realizing it his lips moved in silent prayer.

"Oh God! Where is *my* Billy? Can't you help me find him? I need to see him and Margie bad. Lord, I got to get there in time, I just gotta. My life isn't worth anything without them. Let me find them and take them home with me once more. Just once God. Then I wouldn't care what happened to me. Take my life, but let me have my family back for just a little while. Lord, I ask you in Christ's name. Amen."

Emma Miles was talking to the Simmons downstairs while Roger was praying. After he finished he leaned off the side of the bed to hear their conversation below. Then he peeped through a crack in the floor and he could see her weeping again.

"Arthur was drunk again last night as usual. He'd gotten his pay yesterday morning and after leaving us some money for groceries he went off with those no-good buddies of his. I never saw him alive after that!" Then Mrs. Miles broke into uncontrolled sobbing.

"There, there, honey," comforted Mrs. Simmons. "Why don't you let the rest wait until some other time, don't you want to?"

"No, let me finish. I've got to get it off my mind. And thanks so much for letting me burden you with my troubles. You and Pop have been wonderful. The next time I saw Arthur was this morning in that casket. The undertaker said he had a bullet in his heart. He looked so natural and there was a smile on his face. Oh! what am I going to do without him? What are the kids going to do without their daddy? Oh, Arthur, Arthur. He's gone. He's gone away from me, Oh God help me to stay sane!"

Again Emma broke down and wept without restraint. The Simmons lifted her exhausted body over to the bed and covered her up for the night. Then they dried their eyes and went to bed also.

"Soon everyone was asleep but me and I was living in torment. I knew Hell couldn't be any worse than this. I was in the same house with the wife and children of one of the men I killed. I had to listen to her heartache and see her suffer like that. I was crushed and I felt meaner and dirtier than any man that ever lived. I was planning to get away during the night sometime, but this changed things. How long could I run away from that woman's screaming voice? And how soon could I forget the look on those orphan's faces? No, I couldn't run any more. I thought to myself, nothing could have stunned me more. This was a rotten break."

Roger lay in his bed upstairs for several hours struggling with his conscience and soul. His body writhed and squirmed in agony as he realized more fully how much suffering he had brought to others. An overwhelming sense of guilt surged into his heart and he bit his lips and gnawed at his knuckles until they ran with blood.

"Why did this have to happen anyway? I was doing alright till now. I couldn't help it, I had to kill those fellows. They were hurting me! They'd have killed me if I hadn't got them first. It was self-defense I tell you—it was self-defense."

But Roger couldn't talk himself into escaping from his problem now. He had come face to face with the results of his crime. Three wives and eight children were without bread-winners because of him. This was too much for him so he made up his mind to take his punishment.

"Finally I gave up and a calm settled over me. The confusion and pain in my heart left me. I guess I relaxed for the first time in weeks after making my resolution. I had been acting like a coward and was running away from blame, but I decided to take it now. It couldn't be any worse than what I had just been through. I thought sure I was going crazy there for awhile."

This awakening within Roger gave him new confidence and strength.

"I felt like a real man again. I even respected myself because of the thing I had decided to do. No more running now—I was going to give myself up. It was a hard decision to make, but the way of the transgressor is hard anyway. Neither decision was a pleasant one. So, I boiled all my problems down to just two. First, I had to give myself up without getting shot in the process and the second was to do something for the families I had harmed. I didn't know how I could do the latter, but at least I could try."

"It was after 4:30 a.m. when I slipped out of bed and dressed. Then I crawled down the ladder and awoke the Simmons. Mrs. Miles and the children continued to sleep soundly as we went into the kitchen and lit a fire. The old folks didn't act like they were surprised at my actions so I felt at ease and told them everything. They listened attentively and we all got to crying before I was through. They found it hard to believe that I was the one who had done the killing, but when I told them all the details they were convinced."

The Simmons were pleased and impressed by Roger's new confidence in himself. They saw the faraway look was gone from his eyes and that he moved about with greater poise and direction. They hardly recognized the new Roger as the weakling who had come to their door ten hours before.

"But what do you want us to do Ben, I mean Roger?" asked the old man. "You'll have to excuse us for calling you Ben. But that's what you told us your name was at supper last night."

"I want you to call the police for me. I want you to tell them my side of the story. I don't think they'd listen to me, but they might believe you."

"Mr. Simmons agreed to do as I asked. He quickly dressed and we started off down the road to the all night service station where a telephone was. We didn't say much. I guess he didn't know what to say and I didn't feel like talking at all."

There was a few minutes wait after the call was made to the State Highway Patrol Office. Then police cars came from both directions. The State Highway Patrol, the County Sheriff's men, and some special deputies had been patrolling and searching the area since the killings. They responded to the call immediately. The station driveway was soon crowded with cars and armed police.

"Mr. Simmons told them I was harmless and peaceful but they didn't take any chances. Just like the police and robbers serials in the movies, they stayed behind their cars with their guns ready and told me to come out with my hands up. They weren't taking any chances. They thought they were dealing with some desperado but it was just me. When I went outside they handcuffed me. Then they waited a few minutes while the newspaper reporters took pictures and asked me a few questions. Then they put me in a car and drove me to the city for medical treatment and later confinement."

•

"Shadows had crept into the courtroom now and I could see that the spectators were tired from sitting or standing so long. The Judge looked tired too. Finally, because there were so few witnesses left to be heard, the Judge ruled that the trial would go into night session. He explained to both sides that the court docket was overloaded and that they needed to begin another big trial the next day if possible. So the lawyers speeded up their final plans."

Several character witnesses remained to be heard. Among them was Roger's high school principal from Centerville.

"He was an average boy I would say, or nearly average. His grades weren't too high, but he didn't fail any subjects. I would say he got along with the other students reasonably well. He should have credit for that, because it wasn't easy."

"What do you mean, it wasn't easy?" questioned Roger's attorney.

"Well you see he was a timid kind of boy. Never aggressive. This caused some of the other students to pick on him. You know what I mean, they teased him a lot and heckled him when they could. But he took it well. He was one of the mildest students we had in school at that time. So you can see why the news of his crime was such a shock to our town. Why, he was the last boy in the world we would have expected to do such a thing. He was a fine boy while with us."

Other witnesses followed Mr. Donohoe and said about the same things about Roger. The grocerman, the sheriff and an elder of the church at Centerville testified in his favor. Then the Defense rested its case.

"In many respects my trial was a simple one and turned out not to be as bad as I had feared. The State's attorneys got all the witnesses they could to testify against me and my lawyers got everyone to say nice things about me. Then the lawyers finished their part by giving the jury a summary of the facts. After that was over the Judge instructed the jury on how to reach a fair verdict and then the case was closed. The State's summation contained some passioned pleas in the name of justice and right. They claimed they had proved their first-degree-murder charge and that I should get the extreme penalty."

"Then my lawyers finished their part of the case. They admitted my guilt but challenged the first-degree charge. They said I was only defending myself and that the charge should be manslaughter which would carry with it a lighter sentence. They said they had presented enough circumstantial evidence to prove this contention."

"I sure was glad I wasn't on *that* jury because they had a hard job ahead of them. I could tell that some of them were thoroughly confused and I didn't blame them. At times the lawyers got me confused too. Neither side stayed on the truth all the time. The State tried to make me appear worse than I was and my lawyers tried to convince them that I was a cousin to an angel from Heaven. Sometimes I hardly recognized myself."

"After all the fuss was over the jury was sent to its quarters to deliberate on their verdict. The Judge went back to his room behind the courtroom and the spectators left to get sandwiches and coffee. This left only the guards and me, outside of my close friends and relatives."

"The guard took me to a little room off to the side of the large auditorium and locked me in. My loved ones came to the little barred window and tried to encourage me."

"God knows best. All of you believe that and if you do it will cheer me up more than anything else. Whatever God decides to do with me will be the right thing as far as I'm concerned. If He rules that I should only get imprisonment then I shall accept the verdict with deepest gratitude. But if He thinks I've done too much wrong to be worth anything to the world any longer, then I shall go my way smiling."

Roger's family turned away in tears, but comforted.

"It was black as ebony outside my window now so I couldn't see anything but what was illuminated by the street lights. I stood by my window and looked out for a long time. Occasionally I heard voices coming from the juryroom. I could tell from the pitch of the voices that their debate was rising to a fevered tempo. And the more I listened the more conscious I became that those men were deciding *my* fate. I didn't have anything to do with it anymore. Whether I lived or died depended on those twelve men."

"I stood there awhile longer and then realized how trying the day had been for me too. I was mentally and physically exhausted. So I lay down on the wooden bench and started to pray. My attempts weren't too fruitful at first, but I finally got easier and my mind relaxed some. I still couldn't believe all this. It didn't seem that it could be happening to *me*. How I wished it had been only a horrible nightmare and when I awoke it would be all gone. But such day-dreaming couldn't change the hard, cold facts. It was me and I was in prison. And now I was awaiting the outcome of my trial. This was life in its most realistic form—the time of deep distress."

"How many times had I thought that such things as this could happen to others, but never to me? Yet, it had happened to me, so maybe I didn't have a charmed life after all. Most of us think we do. And my luck hadn't held out either, so I guess I was wrong in trusting to luck in the first place. As a kid I just always figured things would work out alright sooner or later and never spent too much time preparing for life. But now I had learned the price for thinking like that. Because of it I had made some horrible mistakes and now I was a young criminal."

CHAPTER 2

A HOME TO A HOUSE

"WHAT DOES IT TAKE to make a home out of a house? I asked myself. Then I lay there in my cell and tried to figure my riddle out. Someone had said it takes "a heap o' living" and I guess that's right. But what causes the reverse? If I'm logical, the answer is the lack of good living. That's how *our* home changed. It lost the good living in it."

"I wondered a lot about my present trouble. How could I have gotten this far on the other side of the law? I wasn't sure what the correct answer was. Here I was in prison and this in spite of the fact that I never intentionally hurt anyone in my life? Anyway, I decided to take the blame that was coming to me. If I had watched myself more carefully this wouldn't have happened."

"Somewhere down the line something happened to my moral fiber. If I hadn't been weak in character somewhere I would never have gotten into the position where I had to kill those men. But I keep wondering. What influenced me in the wrong direction, without my knowing it?"

It was evident to Roger that he was the victim of circumstances to some extent, but since he had been taught the difference between right and wrong he knew he couldn't put all of the blame on others. It was a lot his too.

"I told myself that I was a different person now to what I had been 12 months before when I thought I could run away from trouble. I was feeling rebellion pretty strong then, but something made me change. What was it that reconciled me to this life of confinement?"

"Then the answer came into my mind clearly. I had learned from the Bible not to resist the police or the laws of the land. In my readings I learned not to challenge the 'higher powers' because they are 'ordained of God' and they 'bear not the sword in vain' when it comes to law violators. I remember the reference now, it was in the 13th chapter of Romans. There I learned that I resisted the power of God when I resisted the government. And that time I was planning to run away, I was trying to run away from God too, but I found out I couldn't."

"But that trial today! That sure was a lot of nonsense to me. They'd have saved themselves a lot of time and money if they'd done what I thought ought to be done. I thought they ought to lock me up for the rest of my life and be done with it. That's what my lawyers told me I should expect at the most."

"I still don't have my answer yet. I don't know what happened to me to lead me into a life of crime, if you can call it that. It all happened in such a short time, but after it was over there was nothing I could do to change it. Maybe if I think back something will come to me."

●

"I remember some things about my first home, though I was quite young when I left there. I can still see it. A little white frame farmhouse about a quarter of a mile from the highway. I feel good every time I think about those first months there. I guess its childish of me, but I swallow kinda hard when I think how beautiful those green gables were. I liked mother's flowers and shrubs too and I got into trouble when I picked them sometimes. But I loved getting in trouble with mother. Those were precious memories and those days turned out to be the only really happy home days I had as a youngster."

"Our home wasn't elaborate in the way of furniture and appliances, but we had enough. I guess you would say it was average or typical. Everybody loved everybody else and other things didn't count much with us. I can still remember the gay times my sisters and I used to have there."

"The girls have changed a lot since then, but to me they'll always be long-legged and awkward kids with stringy hair over their shoulders. That was the way I remembered them last. Then there was my father. I remember mother telling me that our move to the country was for his benefit. She said his health was bad and he needed a change. Of course we kids were all for the move because it gave us more yard in which to play."

Roger was too young, at the age of three, to know the real reason the Scotts left the big city. Mr. Scott had been involved with a gang of gamblers and cheats and he was about to drink himself to death. The doctor ordered the change in hopes that hard work and plenty of healthful exercise might break his acute alcoholism problem.

"I have to grin every time I think about our first year on the farm. I was almost too small to remember anything, but I retained a little. But it was the second year when I was four that I remember a lot more. Then the next year I couldn't forget a thing. That was the year we had such good crops. That old land did itself up right that year. That and daddy's hard work."

"That was by far the happiest year of my whole life as a child. Maybe that's the reason I remember so much about it. There was that Thanksgiving-style turkey dinner with all the trimmings and the gifts after that. When daddy got his checks from the gin we splurged there for a while, but they had earned it. After the meal mother and dad sprung the surprise on us children. Maree got the blue silk dress she had been begging for and Jan got her pink one and Sue got the yellow one. I got a cowboy suit and it was the best to be found in town. I was real proud of it. But that wasn't the sweetest part of it all. It sure made us feel good to watch mother and dad exchange their gifts too. I felt real good and secure inside just watching them sitting in the swing and hugging and kissing each other on the nose."

The gay times at the Scott home were wonderful while they lasted, but they came to a premature end. Ominous clouds of ill-fortune were rolling up behind the horizon. They hadn't hidden the sunlight yet, but the winds of tragedy soon blew them over the Scott place and left a scarred farm and family.

"The next year was that rainy year. Those rain storms started early in the winter and didn't slack up until early May. I remember daddy didn't plant a thing until May that year. And that weather wasn't good on dad either. Seems like he coughed a lot during those months and complained of his chest hurting him.'

The fact was that Mr. Scott's confinement that winter broke his health down to near tuberculosis. And on top of that he had to work extra long hours in the late Spring repairing his ploughs, cultivators and planters. He drove his teams from sunup to dark trying to get caught up and the pressure on the old equipment was taking its toll.

"If the late planting had been his only problem we might have done all right that year. But that old mule got sick and the hired hand ran off, so things got worse rather than better. That was bad too when daddy rammed his arm into that nail at the barn. He was trying to round up the old sow. That laid him up for a couple of extra days. It seemed like ole dame Fortune was working against us that time."

"On and on it went. One thing after another went wrong at our place. Part of the late crop got washed out just as the tender cotton plants were peeking out of the ground. So it was soon evident that we couldn't meet the mortgage note at the bank on time, and maybe not at all."

"Daddy got pretty discouraged after that. They talked a lot about the good crop the year before, but that didn't hold him up for long. That was a good attempt when mother tried to cheer him by telling him that farmers don't expect a good crop but every third year anyhow, but it didn't work so well in our case."

Mr. Scott had made the mistake of putting too much money into seed for this year's planting and he wasn't able to get it in the ground, nor was he able to sell it. Other farmers had all the seed they needed because they were short on planting too.

"Mother made a mistake when she agreed for daddy to go to the city alone to get our bank loan refinanced. She ought to have known he would run into some of his old buddies, but she was a trusting wife. Somehow he never got to the bank. They got hold of him first and loaned him enough money to get by on for awhile. Later he found out that the loan was a trap and that they intended to force him back into their shady business. Of course mother suspected this the minute she heard where the money came from, but there wasn't much she could do then. He had already spent about half of it."

"Things picked up around the Scott farm for awhile after that. Our machinery was repaired or replaced and a new mule was bought. Finally daddy got his planting finished and began helping mother with the garden canning. We children had a gay time running the fresh vegetables from the garden to the house for processing and canning. Momentarily our homelife returned to normal. It looked as though we might make out after all.

"Just when we were sitting pretty those insects had to come along. First the boll-weevil and then the grasshoppers. Those hoppers sure were big that year; they could jump almost six feet without much trouble. It was a hard battle but with the help of some kind of spray daddy saved some of the crops. However, we didn't have much left after paying all expenses. And there was that bill to the gamblers. Guess mother must have been awfully upset about that. She sure dared those men to set a foot on our place."

However, Mrs. Scott didn't do much when the gamblers drove up one night about dark. "We come to see your husband, Mrs. Scott," one man shouted from the car.

"He's not here. What do you want?"

"We come to collect some money he owes us. Do you want to pay us or shall we come back?"

"You'll have to come back. I'll tell him you were here."

"Tell him to come in to see us tomorrow or we'll be back tomorrow night, see?" With this the thugs whirled the car around and sped down the dirt road to the highway leaving a large cloud of dust behind.

"The next day the gamblers told daddy they had been losing heavily in their operations and wanted their money then—with interest. They were told that they could have the 15% interest now, but that the principle would have to wait awhile longer. So they refinanced his loan and the interest rate went to 20%. Daddy knew he was at the mercy of these men but he didn't know how to keep from getting in deeper with them."

"Then came daddy's big mistake. What ever possessed him to think he could win at the gambling tables? Anyway he went back to town with all the money we had left and lost it all on the roulette wheel. And as if that wasn't bad enough, these men cornered him and demanded full payment of our debt to them. When they found out he couldn't pay they surprised him by inviting him to have some drinks with them."

When Mr. Scott arrived home early the next morning he was on the verge of derangement. His last attempt at a solution to their problems had failed miserably and now the syndicate in the city was going to file suit against him for their money. They told him they would have a judgment against his farm in a few days.

"After this daddy began to stay away from home a lot. We never knew where he went or what he did, but he was never the same after that. I guess he had given up. That was the contrast between him and mother. She was still in there fighting. It looked hopeless, but she kept trying to figure out something. Now I know that it was only through her efforts that the family had stayed together this long. I don't know what they said in that later discussion they had, but it didn't seem to help us out much."

When the discussion between the Scotts was over, both knew that little had been accomplished. They talked throughout the night and though several things were agreed upon, nothing lasting was in sight. As a last resort Mrs. Scott tried to enforce a reform program on her husband. She knew the chances of it working weren't great. She had to act as his will now—since he had none left. Some agreements had been made, such as his promise to try harder to make the farm pay itself out. Too, they agreed to try to maintain a better atmosphere around the house for the children's sake. But the contract was superficial at best and was doomed for certain failure. With the basis for genuine respect between the two almost gone, it was evident that some drastic changes were due in the Scott household—soon.

"We kids sure did feel scared when mama and daddy finished their talking that morning. It was dark and misty all day which made everything seem even worse. The fog rolled in a little after dawn and the dark clouds hung low until mid-afternoon when the torrents of rain began to fall. Since the atmosphere was chilly we children stayed in our room most of the day. I guess everybody in the house was depressed. It was then that our home started slipping badly."

"The worst part of it came two days later. The men from the city came out and took daddy into town with them. He stayed gone all morning and nearly got back too late for dinner. But the dinner part didn't matter."

"Dad came home very drunk. He could hardly keep his feet on the little bridge across the gully in front of our house. Mother was at a neighbor's house to borrow some baking powder and was just leaving when she saw daddy struggling to get up our front porch steps. She started running as soon as she saw him but she was too late to stop him from coming into our bedroom. He busted in and asked us where we kept our butter and egg money. Mama let us save a little money out of the produce we sold sometimes. It was ours and we were saving it to buy Christmas presents in December. Daddy had the wildest look in his eyes and we got real scared of him. I remember I wanted to get under the bed quick, but I was afraid he would come under after me. I guess I didn't do anything but just stand there with my mouth open."

"Daddy was rummaging through our dresser drawers when mother rushed into the room. She suspected what he was up to and was determined that we would not get another penny of our money for liquor. Finally, daddy found our savings in a drawer.

"Albert Scott! put that money back where you got it!" Mrs. Scott demanded with great determination.

"Now you stay out of this, Lona," he said, "I'm dry as a bone and gotta get something to wet my whistle. Just a little is all I need. Go way and leave me 'lone."

"Mother charged at daddy like a tigress defending her cubs against a panther. 'Give me that sack of money! Turn loose of it Albert.' And with a quick motion she wrested it from his hands."

"Now listen to me, Lona, I come to get this money and I aims to have it. I made it. Its mine, so git away. And give me my money!"

Twice daddy lunged at the paper sack containing our money and both times mother was too quick for him. Now his temper was rising and he doubled up his fist and struck mother a crushing blow in the face. She fell limp and hit the floor hard as blood began to run out of her nose and mouth."

35

"Oh God, I pray that I'll never have to go through another experience like that. All of us kids were terrified! We saw it all. I think the girls ran out of the room after that, I don't remember. I was so scared I couldn't think. I thought he had killed my mother and I hated him right there. I made up my mind too. If he had killed my mother I was going to do something awful to him for it."

"The girls came back into the room with a wet towel and began to bathe mother's face. Daddy just stood there hump-shouldered and glaring down at mother. To our relief she finally regained consciousness."

"Get out of this house, Albert! Get out of here and don't ever put your foot on this place again. You don't deserve a wife and kids. You couldn't take care of a home if you had one. Now get out of my sight!"

"A twenty-pound hammer couldn't have hurt daddy worse than those words from mother. I looked into his eyes and I cried hard. He was the most pitiful-looking man I ever saw. I saw hurt in his eyes—he was hurt bad. After that he fell down by mother and begged her to give him another chance. He promised to quit drinking and stay on the place more and treat us children better, but mother's ears were deaf to him. I turned my head when he got up and stumbled out of the house. We never saw him again. We never knew what happened to him."

"Mother filed for a divorce the next time she went to town. She got it in a few months and tried to settle down on the farm to making us children a living. But it wasn't long until it was evident she couldn't. The hired help wasn't efficient and she couldn't manage the farm and do all of her house work too, so she soon realized that something else would have to be worked out."

"I've done everything I can to keep us together, she told us, we just can't make it this way. Now I've arranged for Maree and Jan to go to Uncle Bob's in Oregon and Sue, you're to stay with cousin Ruby in North Carolina for awhile."

"I frowned when mother turned her attention to me. I was afraid she wouldn't tell me I was going with her, and sure enough she didn't. I was being sent to my Grandpa and Grandma Horton's place."

36

" 'You'll like Centerville, Roger,' she reassured me. 'Grandpa Horton has some horses and cows and you can ride and play about the place and have the best time.' "

"But I don't want to go, mama! I don't want to go anywhere! I want to go with you, please, please, let me stay with you!"

"Maree, Jan and Sue left for their new homes the day after being told about mother's new plan."

" 'Honey, I know it's a heartbreaking experience for you right now, but mama will come for you soon. Now you be a good boy on the train and Grandma and Grandpa Horton will meet you at the station this afternoon. Now remember, don't get off the train at any of the stops.' So I was put on a train also."

"Mama, I don't want to go. I don't want to go without you. I'll do anything, but don't send me away. Please don't mama, please don't!" But my pleas went unheeded. Mother was sobbing as she turned loose of my hand, but she felt that this was best for me."

"That was another episode in my life that I've never gotten over. I was so lonely and depressed that leaving mother was more than I could stand. I think after that I just buried my face in my hands and cried and cried."

CHAPTER 3

GROWING PAINS

"To say i was scared on that train by myself would be a great understatement. I was panicky! It was my first time to be away from mother and I was utterly lost. And to add to my misery I wasn't sure I could recognize my grandparents at Centerville. They had never approved of daddy so we never visited each other but once. I didn't cry *all* the way but it was a struggle to keep from it. These were situations I had never been in before and there was no one along to help me."

"I was somewhat relieved when the train pulled into the Centerville station. I put my nose against the window and peered out at everybody on the platform. I didn't see my folks anywhere. I guess I looked real funny with my nose flattened against that window; everybody that saw me laughed. The more I looked the more bewildered I became. The folks weren't anywhere in sight. I thought maybe my greatest dread was coming true. There were all kinds of people out there; short and tall ones, fat and skinny ones, but none that looked like the Hortons. For some reason the depot was unusually crowded that day and others were rushing up to the crowd all the time. That really frightened me. I knew I couldn't find my folks in a crowd like that. My heart sure was pumping fast."

"As soon as I dared, I jumped out of my seat and squirmed through the people and finally reached the vestibule. Just as I reached the door a brass band began to play 'Dixie.' People everywhere began to shout and wave banners and throw hats and paper into the air. For a minute there I forgot all my worries as I enjoyed the show."

"I wondered what this was all about and thought for a minute it might be for me. But then I couldn't figure why they would

38

go to all this fuss just for one little boy. For a second I hesitated; what would I say to all those people? But my fears were soon banished. A large man's form overshadowed me as he shoved his way through the isle and down the train steps. When he stepped off the train more signs went up and the people cheered until it was a deafening roar. Through the noise I heard a chorus of 'Welcome home, Senator!' "

"Presently the band got in front of the Senator's car and the crowd started marching toward the courthouse square where this man was scheduled to make a speech."

"The conductor on the train waved to the engineer in the locomotive cab and shouted for the last time, 'All aboard!' The train slowly moved out of the station and disappeared around the bend."

"The music from the band was getting softer now and I could tell the crowd was nearly wherever it was going. In another five minutes the depot was deserted except for the agent and one frightened little boy—me. The old agent shoved cases and crates around the platform for a few minutes longer. He put a lot of freight in the store room and after locking up the Railway Express office started off to town. But out of the corner of his eye he spied me."

"Well now, what's this? What are you doing out here all by yourself young man? Where's your folks?"

"They're not here yet."

"What's their name sonny? Maybe I know them."

"Their name is Horton. I call my grandfather, Grandpa Horton. Do you know him?"

"Horton, Horton. That name rings a bell. Now let's see. There's a Horton that lives just outside of the city limits on the end of Mulberry street. Or is his name Norton?"

"I don't know where my grandfather lives, sir. But could you take me to him?"

"I can if that's him, son, but maybe that ain't him. You sure you're off at the right town? This is Centerville. Is this where you wanted to get off?"

"This froze me! Suppose I *had* gotten off at the wrong town. What would I do next?"

"Lucky for me, however, my fears were shortlived. A rickety old ford's engine broke the silence, much to my relief as it headed into the station parking lot. The kindly-looking old couple looked kinda like my grandpa and grandma, so I was relieved."

"Welcome to Centerville, Roger. Dad and me have been real anxious for you to get here. Now, now what are you crying for?"

"Then grandmother took me in her arms and hugged me close to her breast and then she smiled into my tear-filled eyes. I smiled a little too."

"We're sorry we were late Roger, but Grandmother and me had quite a time getting through that parade downtown. But its alright now."

"We're really happy to see you son," said Grandpa Horton, "and we'll have some real fun together. Just you wait and see. You're going to like Centerville just fine. Yes sir. Now let me get your bags and we'll start home. Hope we don't get stuck in that parade again."

"Grandpa Horton's out-dated jalopy chugged, jerked and sputtered into the street. We drove down main street and passed the attentive crowd gathered around the square. The Senator was shouting a list of his achievements in Congress during the last session. Once out of the business district it was not a long ride out to the Horton's place at the city limits. An aging dog greeted us as we approached the driveway. He managed to emit a few half-hearted barks and wag his lazy tail several times. I knew right off I was going to like ole Jeff. He came to me the first time I called his name."

"The Horton's home wasn't expensive, but it did look comfortable, and what I needed then was some comfort. There were two old rope swings in the side yard which cheered me some. However, their children had been gone from home for several years. Each had married and moved to the big city. The swings hadn't been used in some time, but they were still good and strong. My room was in the northeast corner of the house. It had been Jay's, the Horton's youngest son, before he went off to college."

Grandma Horton was an excellent cook in her own rights and learned several of Roger's pet dishes in the letter she had received from her daughter. She prepared the first treat on the list and asked Roger if he knew what was in the letter his mother sent. He didn't, of course, so she read him the list of good things his mother had suggested would please him. And when the chicken-pot pie was placed in the center of the table little Roger felt a little more at home.

"Roger, will you offer thanks for us?" Grandma Horton asked.

"Huh! What's that?"

"Didn't your mother or father teach you to offer thanks at the table at home, son?" Grandma Horton asked.

"No'am, I guess they haven't taught me that. What's it for?"

Both the Hortons were disappointed that Roger had not been given better spiritual training.

"'Well, where does our food come from, son?' asked my grandfather."

"Out of the ground I reckon!"

"And who made the ground, Roger?"

"God did I guess. Is that right?"

"Yes, that's right. God made it. He made everything, that's why we offer thanks when we go to the table. We show our gratitude to Him for our daily blessings. Now bow your head and I'll lead it this time, but you be listening and soon you can lead prayer too. Our Father in Heaven. We thank Thee for this food and the many other good things which have come from Thee this day. We are grateful for health and strength and every providential blessing. Forgive us our sins and continue to watch over us and guide us through the paths of righteousness. We ask these things in the name of Christ. Amen."

Roger's first full day at the Horton's drug by slowly. There wasn't anything for him to do and he was accustomed to being busy. Mr. Horton worked on the flivver part of the day while Roger watched.

"Where did all of those parts come from, granddaddy?"

"They all came out of this here motor, son. They're all different sizes and shapes aren't they? But they all belong somewhere."

"Can you get them all back in that little motor, grandpa?"

"Yep, guess I can. Just sit tight on that fender and I'll have them all back in place in a jiffy."

41

"And sure enough, when Grandpa got through, all the parts had disappeared."

"Now let's go try it out, what do you say?"

"And after Grandpa tightened all the cylinder bolts we got into the car and drove downtown. The car shook in all four directions at once, so I didn't trust it and kept a firm grip on my seat."

"There now, how does that sound? Better, eh? That big knock is gone. Sounds pretty smooth and quiet to me. How about you son?"

"It doesn't sound very quiet to me. I don't know whether that knock is gone or not. I can't tell one knock from the other."

"In a few weeks I got better acquainted around Centerville. And when I made a few friends and had some playmates I was much better satisfied. But one day, after having been there about a month, I went in the house with a frown on my face. I wanted to ask a question."

"What's the matter, Roger?"

"Grandma, when's my mother coming to get me? I'm lonesome without her."

"She'll come for you before too long, honey, now you just be as patient as you can. Go out and play some more."

"I was patient. I thought I was extra-patient for a little boy my age. But when weeks continued to fly by and the months rolled by I couldn't restrain myself any longer. I began to cry a lot and broke into tears at the slightest provocation. They told me several different things trying to stall for time, but none of their explanations satisfied me for long."

"I turned seven years old during my second year with my grandparents. I was scheduled to enroll in grammar school, but I didn't want to without my mother. However, a number of my neighborhood friends were starting to school also, so I didn't dread the new experience too much after all."

"My first day at school was awful as well as disappointing. Things got in a tangle and never did get straightened out. First of all, I lost the note Grandma Horton sent to the teacher. That surely was an embarrassing situation."

"What is your name, young man?"

42

"I'm Roger Scott, mam."

"And what's your middle name or initial?"

"I don't know. I don't guess I have one."

"You don't know your middle name? What kind of a child are you? Where is your mother? I'll ask her."

"I don't know where she is, mam, she hasn't written me lately."

"No, no, that's not what I mean. Who is at school with you today?"

"Nobody. I came with some of my neighbors. My grandma sent you a note but I guess I lost it."

"You guess you lost it! You bad boy. Hurry up, this line is long, now where is your note?"

"I was mortified when I couldn't find my note. I was standing in front of the class and was getting a strong tongue lashing from this not-so-understanding teacher."

"I'm not sure whether the teacher was to blame or not, but the class sure got a bad impression of me that day. And the smarty, who made fun of me because I didn't have a mother or daddy, didn't help my reputation. Once the class got to giggling at me I thought they'd never stop. It was very embarrassing!"

"I was relieved when recess came and everyone went out on the playground. The children formed in groups, as is natural and some coupled up. But no one came around me. This made me feel very funny. I felt inferior to the others and this feeling raised serious doubts in my mind as to whether I was welcome at this school or not. No one seemed anxious to have me around. But this was only the beginning! The others at school learned that I was quiet and even-tempered and they took advantage of my good nature and poured on the teasing. They didn't mean any real harm, but they created some attitudes in me that later played a major part in my crime. The older boys went even farther. Three of them threatened to catch me after school some day and beat me up, while others only picked at me to see me flinch. This behavior, added to my loneliness, crushed my spirits. I lost my self-confidence."

"I finally got over those first trials, but they were rough. And I became a good student, much to my own surprise. I stayed in the upper 25% of my class for a long time. I tried to impress the teacher and some of my classmates, but my scheme didn't work. I hoped some of the class would look up to me for my scholastic ability, but I was disappointed. If I made good grades the dumber students didn't like me. If I let my grades drop some to please them, then the better students heckled me. That old jinx just wasn't to be broken. After that I didn't know what to do to influence people or win friends."

"As the months went by I kept my school grades consistently good, but I made little social progress. I found out that an education without the ability to get along with people wasn't worth much. I shyed away from the other students most of the time. I guess it was because they stayed away from me. The tale went all through the school that I had been deserted by my folks and that no one wanted me. I even heard that my grandparents wished they could get rid of me. Later, I learned that this was a lie, but I suffered misery while I believed it."

"The closest friend I had was Charlie. His parents were poor and he wore ragged clothes to school, but they were always clean and neatly ironed. Charlie and I had a lot in common. Neither of us was accepted by the class. We felt this keenly too, but we only confided our disappointments in each other. Neither of us knew anything to do to get into the good graces of our classmates. We were two of a kind; not generally accepted, and for no good reason."

"In many ways I was happy in my foster home. I had a measure of love and affection and I certainly had security. But I never fully felt that I belonged there. My grandfather was a busy man. He was successful in his business and had saved a lot of money. He could well afford to bear the expense of rearing me, but that wasn't all I needed. However, I guess that was one reason mother didn't mind leaving me with them. She knew I would be given good care. But I wasn't given the kind of care I needed. Only my mother could have given me that. I needed to be loved and coddled. I needed someone to tell me how much I was loved and how important I was to them. But I never got this at all. My grandparents were good to me, but there was always a barrier between us. I think it was our age difference. They had forgotten how to rear children and they starved me emotionally. I had plenty of good homemade biscuits every day, but what I needed was the bread of human kindness."

"Time changed many things in Centerville and I was one of them. I noticed changes coming on. As I grew older I learned to think for myself more and I felt more independent and capable of working out my own problems. Of course, this was true only in instances, but I thought I could handle anything. Too, I felt like one of the family now at the Horton's and I didn't hesitate to cross grandpa's wishes if I didn't agree with him on things."

"I guess my problem grew steadily worse as I became belligerent about mother's neglect of me. I thought I had stayed at the Horton's long enough and I didn't appreciate all the mystery about mother. They were keeping me in the dark about something and I knew it, but I couldn't get them to tell me what it was all about. And the more I thought about the matter the angrier I got inside. I guess I must have really tried myself. At least I made life miserable for the folks there for awhile."

"This is terrible punishment on Roger," Grandma Horton told her husband. "Why can't we just come right out and tell him his mother has deserted him? What's wrong with doing that?"

"If you tell Roger something like that now there's no telling what he'll do. He'd run away sure. No! I think its too risky to tell him now. Maybe later," replied Grandpa Horton.

"About a year and a half after I went to the Horton's, they got a letter from my mother. They had been expecting a letter from her with my train ticket in it, but that wasn't what they got. Instead, there was a short note:

"Dear Mom and Dad,

Probably you won't appreciate this, but I'm getting married again and I just must ask you to keep Roger awhile longer. We want to enjoy our honeymoon and then get settled down and then I will send for him. Give him my love.

Bert is such a nice man. We work in the same office. I just couldn't turn his proposal down. He's tall, handsome and has a good future with the company here.

You will forgive me for this short delay won't you? After all, I am still a young woman and I'm entitled to a little more pleasure out of life before I settle down with the children again.

If Roger continues to give you trouble punish him the best way you see fit.

Love,

Lona."

"She doesn't realize what she's asking," said Grandpa Horton. "This boy is nearly eight now and he's getting harder to manage all the time. I don't know what's gotten into that boy. I don't think any of our boys behaved like that. What are we going to do with him?"

"I don't know, dad. We've kept putting the child off until I'm ashamed to face him any more. And I'm doubly ashamed of Lona. What ever possessed her do you reckon? Why has she done so strangely about the children? We didn't rear our children that way did we? This situation is becoming unbearable! We've got to do something to satisfy Roger. He's going to drive us all crazy, including himself."

"My grandparents later told me that the time came and went for mother to write for me to come to her. She had her honeymoon and went back to her work there. My folks wrote her several times and wired her. Finally they called her long-distance but they couldn't find her then. She had moved and didn't leave a forwarding address."

"Mother's disappearance created a worse problem for my grandparents. They didn't know of any way to explain the situation to me. They couldn't just come right out and tell me my own mother had deserted me. It nearly worried them to death."

"Now mama, you just watch! One of these days Roger's going to force a showdown and its going to be awfully hard explaining the situation. I wish Lona hadn't misbehaved that way. She could make things so much easier."

"It was the following Saturday night that I did force the issue. I was so upset and irritable that I didn't care what I did."

"I want to know where my mother is! I want to go to her

right now. If you don't tell me I'll find her myself. Why hasn't she written me, or come to get me? She promised she would. She promised!"

"This put the folks in a very awkward spot. What could they tell me? Your mother has gotten married and won't be back for you? She doesn't want you? Yes, they could have told me the hard truth, but neither could bear the thought of hurting me that much. I was already heartsick from loneliness and yearning for my mother. And they were right! It would have been the death blow if they had told me the true facts then."

"Dad, I don't know what to do! I'd rather do almost anything than tell that blessed little thing that he isn't wanted. He must be wanted. Lona must be mixed up. Surely she'll come for him after all."

"But what are we going to do in the meantime? How are you going to pacify Roger? For all we know she may be dead."

"At this moment I entered the room. I heard the last few words spoken by my grandfather."

"Dead? Did you say my mother was dead, grandpa? Tell me, please! Is that why she hasn't come for me? Has my mother died?"

"Now take it easy, son." Grandpa Horton said. "You may not have understood me just right. That's not exactly what I said."

"Then you mean she's dying somewhere. Where is she? I want to go to her. I want to go now!"

"You can't go to your mother child, we don't know where she is. We tried to find her but haven't been able to. You see. . . ."

"I broke into the conversation. 'Then she is dead! She's not coming back to get me. She isn't is she?'"

"Neither of the Horton's knew what to say at this point. I had gotten an impression which they could neither prove nor disprove."

"Son, we don't know where your mother is." said Grandpa Horton.

"You don't know how it happened; where she's buried or none of that?"

"No child, your grandfather and I can't locate her. She *may be* dead. We just don't know. That is . . . Oh, I don't know how to put it."

"Then she is dead, grandma! She is dead! You're just trying to keep it from me. Please tell me about it. When did she die?"

"My grandparents were really in a jam now and didn't know how to get out of it. I had the impression that mother was dead and that they were trying to keep it from me. I misunderstood everything they said after that."

"I remember rushing back into my room and falling across my bed and crying for hours. I was convinced that my mother was dead. I thought the Hortons were just trying to spare my feelings. But the news broke my heart anyway. Nothing mattered to me for a long time after that. The folks tried to straighten the matter out several times but I never gave them a chance. I wouldn't talk to them about anything for weeks. So I went on believing my mother was dead, and this killed all my hopes of being happy again. My whole world had been built around my return to mother. I had dreamed and played make-believe for three years expecting to go back to her. But my fondest dreams turned out to be in vain. They burst like a soap bubble and left me a frustrated kid."

"For months after this episode I was listless. I ate little and didn't care what happened to me at home or at school. The Hortons kept trying to contact mother, but they never succeeded. No news came."

"My picture of mother was the most valuable treasure I had left. I thought she was the most beautiful lady in the world. In her I saw all the love and purity and tenderness which graces the race of woman. Until now I had tried to pattern my life after all the good qualities I had remembered in her; courage, patience and understanding. But those things didn't matter to me much any more. Mother was gone. I remember I used to sit and talk to the picture and imagine that mother was talking back to me. It comforted me just to play like she was talking to me. I felt that she was the only person who could really understand me and my childish problems. There was some small consolation in knowing that I would get to see my

48

sisters occasionally, but it wasn't like having my mother back."

"My school work fell off drasticly after this. I barely passed my subjects. The teachers got real concerned and reported me to the principal."

"We don't know what to think of that boy. He was doing just fine until a few weeks ago. Now he doesn't care. We've scolded him and praised him and threatened him. Nothing does any good."

"No one but the Horton's and me knew the real cause for my sudden change for the worse. This was an embarressing situation for them and they weren't talking about it to anyone."

"The school teachers soon gave up trying to do anything with me. They adopted a general hands-off policy. I guess they thought they could line me up by ignoring me."

"What I needed at this time was a sympathetic love and some understanding. With mother gone I felt that no one loved me. Grandmother had tried to take mother's place, but it was never a satisfactory arrangement. She didn't understand me as well as mother would have. My teachers could have helped me too and also my classmates, but instead of getting closer to me when I needed help they got farther from me. If I could have had just one teacher who would have taken me as a pet project and listened to my troubles, I might have pulled out of my problem faster. But my self-consciousness and timidity got worse instead of better."

"Eventually school became an almost unbearable experience for me. Before I got readjusted to my new thoughts about mother, the principal called me into his office and criticized me about my grades. But he soon saw that criticism didn't help. He then tried other approaches but I wouldn't tell him anything, so he finally gave up. He dismissed me from his office without learning anything new."

"When Grandpa realized that they were stuck with me for good, he changed his attitude toward me. He got much stricter. He was afraid they wouldn't rear me right and the responsibility bore down on his mind. He threatened me a lot more and his temper flared whenever I didn't do everything just like he ordered it. I dreaded this new situation, but there wasn't anything I could do about it."

"Grandma talked constantly to keep Grandpa from whipping me so much for small things I did, but that didn't help either. Everyone's nerves was on edge and this job was too much for Grandpa at his age."

"How well I recall those lickings. I remember I was determined not to say a word back. That always baffled Grandpa. He'd always shake his head after he whipped me and I refused to cry. I just sulked. But his punishment didn't hurt me much then. I wasn't feeling anything. I had lost my mother and I was still numb and I didn't care what happened to me."

"Now that years have passed since those whippings, its clear that Grandpa's approach was all wrong. Instead of creating a fear and a respect in me, he aroused a deep resentment. I never trusted him after that."

"Those whippings behind the shed got into a vicious cycle. The more Grandpa spanked me the more unwanted I felt and the more I pouted. Then the more sullen I got the more he whipped me. He thought he could beat the meanness out of me, but he didn't understand. I wasn't mean. I was confused. I needed understanding and sympathy, not physical punishment. I didn't mind just the whippings at all. I thought those were necessary, but I did resent the unnecessary number of spankings and the severity of some of them. It was during that time that I began to feel that the world was a cold and hard place in which to live."

"The whole community had me marked now as the number one mystery. No one could figure me out; none of them asked me about my trouble either. Some intimated that maybe I wasn't all there, while others were more charitable. They looked on me as just another unfortunate kid."

"But these attitudes of the people in Centerville were no mystery to me. A child can read an adult's face. I knew exactly what they were thinking. I could see that they resented me and I determined to resent them back. That's what caused me to act so independently. I felt that I was another of those persons who had just missed out in life somewhere. I was convinced that I was destined to travel the roads of failure and misfortune alone. Sure enough I was right."

"One person in Centerville could have changed my whole world with just a few little kind deeds but no one sympathized with me. It was me against the world. Had I known one close friend and poured out my heart to him once in awhile, I don't think I would have stored up so many hard feelings against people. But I didn't think my grandparents realized my problem or they wouldn't have repremanded me so much. They would have tried to talk with me more and together we could have worked out some solutions. But once that freedom to talk was gone, we had no means of communication left."

"I guess I developed into a real problem for the folks after that. I felt bad a lot of the time and wanted to do things for no good reason at all. One scrape came after the other and I never did seem to know when to quit. I felt aggressive and wanted to do something; anything, whether it was right or wrong."

"Some of my trouble at home came because I had too much leisure time. There wasn't anything constructive to do around the house. I could do my afternoon chores in an hour and after that I had several hours to kill before supper."

"There were some days when I didn't even come home in time to do my work. I stopped off once to help Eddie fix his fence and another time to help Bob paint his bicycle. Then I went to the park all I could and watched the ball teams play. I got tired of the old routine of just going home and doing nothing. But Grandma was understanding most of the times I was late. I only wish Grandpa had stopped with a scolding."

"Grandpa Horton was at his wit's end. He didn't know what to do with his mischievous grandson. When he got home from work he was usually tired and he didn't feel like disciplining me. He had long since forgotten how he used to rush home from work and take *his* boys hunting or fishing for an hour or so before supper. He enjoyed those things then, but the idea never seemed to cross his mind concerning *me*."

"Grandpa surely got angry at Mr. Wilson, our principal, when he brought me home one afternoon. I was a very dejected boy and guilt must have been written all over my face. Bert and I had broken into the school building after hours and had a big eraser fight in the English room. We used the chalk for machine gun bullets and the erasers as bombs. We spotted the walls and blackboards up pretty bad, but no real damage was done. Mr. Wilson explained to Grandpa that a quarter would pay for the broken chalk. He didn't recommend punishment this time, to my surprise. He told Grandpa to get me a hobby of some kind or some afternoon interests to keep my hands and mind busy. I thought he had a real good idea, but Grandpa didn't."

"Thank you, Mr. Wilson, but I can handle my grandson alright in my own way. He doesn't need a work shop, he just needs his hide tanned!"

"And he really cleaned my plough! He was pretty tired of my shenanigans so he poured it on. I couldn't keep from crying that time. I was black and blue for weeks."

"This extreme punishment was hard on me, but not nearly so bad as the later punishment from my schoolmates. They played all kinds of jokes and tricks on me to tantalize me that week. They had heard about my whipping from Grandpa and they were rubbing it in."

"The kids didn't mean any real harm I'm sure, but they sure made life miserable for me for awhile. Some of their jokes went too far and hurt me deep. I didn't fight back because I had few enough friends as it was. Besides, fighting hadn't settled anything before."

"I felt less wanted in Centerville with each additional episode. I worried so much at times that I thought of running away. Once I thought seriously of suicide."

"I thought I could make everyone feel sorry for me when I was gone, but suicide never really appealed to me. At times I got so depressed, however, that I believe death would have been easier than the suffering I was having. But this self-pity soon wore thin and I went on about my business."

"My conduct after this didn't improve much because most circumstances were working against improvement. I didn't feel that I was being treated right. I was setting my philosophy of life during that time and it wasn't a very pretty one. I was constantly in a state of uncertainty and mental confusion. I never knew what was coming next, so I decided to obey my folks as best I could and then get out on my own as soon as possible. I was thinking of getting as far from Centerville as I could. I didn't want anybody telling *me* what to do."

"That was big talk for a youngster my age, but I was dead serious. Life was being very hard on me and I made up my mind then to put up a real struggle."

CHAPTER 4

ROGER MAKES A CHANGE

"BY NOW I had pretty well convinced myself that the world had given me a raw deal in life. My experiences in high school were no exception. My graduation from grammar school and enrollment in high school forced many changes into my usual routine. I didn't like them. For several years I had taken the same paths to school, but now I was forced to go through another part of town. This brought me into contact with new and strange people and places. I was once again ill-at-ease. I didn't understand why these new experiences should irritate me so, but now I know that I was resenting the breaking of old habits. I was in a rut and felt some security in it, but these new conditions were painful."

"It was true. Through this period of readjustment I had a very unpredictable temperament. I was a disappointed child and wanted others to leave me alone. But there was another reason for my desire for seclusion. When I had tried to make friends and be somebody at grammar school I failed miserably, and I guess I never rose above it. I had failed once and now I was afraid to try again."

"The later hazing at Centerville High didn't add to my courage. The upperclassmen got a great kick out of embarressing us freshmen. They put us through their traditional antics. Our first morning was spent in the high school auditorium with the Superintendent taking most of the time. He told us new students what to expect in the way of classroom order, school discipline and report card grades. He caused a big giggle in the studentbody when he told us we could expect complete cooperation from the upperclassmen."

"Right in the middle of this orientation speech I was brought to shame. I already felt insignificant, sitting among those hundreds of new faces, but I didn't know I was to be the victim of a well-planned trick. I was gullible and took directions from the ushers and they put me in the section of the auditorium where they wanted me. This caused the students in that section to keep looking at me out of the corner of their eyes. I wondered why."

"But I didn't wonder long. And I will never forget how embarrassed I was. The upperclassman had put me in the senior section deliberately. Then some funny guy yelled out, 'there's a freshmen in the senior section, teacher!' When everyone turned around and looked at me I blushed until my face turned as red as a new-polished apple. This stopped the whole program. I sheepishly got up and worked my way down the row and another usher showed me to my place. So there I was—starting off wrong again. The thing I had feared most came true and the studentbody never let me forget it."

"Mr. Donohoe, the Superintendent, continued his speech after the audience got quiet again. He assured us freshmen that the juniors and seniors were reliable guides. He urged us to look to them for help instead of crowding into the office for information."

"I tried to comply with the Superintendent's instructions so I worked his plan. I couldn't find my home room so I asked a junior where room 202 was. He smiled broadly, like a lion about to eat a rabbit, and took great pains to give me directions. He told me to go to the elevator at the end of the hall, where the two big doors were. There I was to get in line until the operator came down and took us to the second floor of the building. The room I wanted was to be the first room on the left from the elevator. The boy seemed like a regular fellow so I thanked him and followed his advice. I liked everything about him but that last smile of his."

"I went down the hall and got in line as the boy told me. I made number twelve in the line. The freshmen were all talking and laughing about how the advanced students weren't going to trick them. They commented on the novelty of having elevator service in their new high school."

"I was as simple-minded as the rest. I thought we were standing before the school elevator too. But when the doors opened everyone pushed forward and almost shoved three of them down some concrete steps. To our surprise and dismay there was no elevator. There were only some steps and a ramp leading down into the boilerroom. The operator laughed heartily since he was in on the joke. He looked into our bewildered faces and sent us on to class."

"Sorry kids, there ain't no elevator here. This is the control room. But don't feel bad about it. You're the fourth batch I've sent away today. Now you'd all better hurry to class. Use those stairs over there."

"And we did hurry too. We were at least ten minutes late now and all of us were afraid we would be sent to the office for being tardy."

"After this second embarrassing incident I became skeptical. When I finally found my home room I caused quite a stir in my attempt to explain why I was late. The class laughed at me and made me feel very small. I was afraid they thought I was stupid. But the teacher came to my rescue and explained, in my defense, that many freshmen fell for that old gag every year."

"I thought I wouldn't get caught in any more traps after this, but I wasn't as smart as I thought. We had been told to locate our lockers before leaving the building that first day and bring our lunches and school supplies to put in them the next day. So I went to the lockerroom. I was stopped by a big senior football player who pushed his chest out at me real big."

"Where are you going, punk? Where's your locker permit?"

"That caught me by surprise. I didn't know what to say, so I didn't say anything. I just stood there dumbfounded."

"Your locker permit, bud, your locker permit! Where is it?"

"He motioned to me to go to the office."

"You'll have to get a permit before getting in here. There's the office. They don't cost nothing, so get one. Don't you know the rules around here?"

"The lady at the desk was awfully busy with a long line of

students and she frowned at me when I told her what I wanted. She put her hands on her hips and really hit the ceiling."

"Another one! How many of you dumb kids are coming in here with that question today? Don't you ever use your heads? You don't need a locker permit, so get out of here, we're busy."

"When I returned to the lockerroom the guard was gone and the halls were empty. When I left school I saw that guy on the playground playing basketball."

"Those jokes sure gave those seniors a big time, but they made us freshmen feel uncomfortable for awhile. For days after that I distrusted everyone. What I was afraid of was that I might get into serious trouble this way."

"My third week of school was becoming more pleasant because the hazing was dying out. By now we freshmen were so skeptical that we even failed to get some lesson assignments, thinking they were jokes."

"Just as I was letting my guard down they pulled another joke on me. A senior in my study hall class told me that all students who made "A" on any morning examination during the first month of school could take the rest of the day off. She said it was a very old school tradition. So, like a sucker, I studied my algebra overtime the night before and made the grade on my morning paper. Then when the 10:30 bell rang I went fishing."

"When I got home that afternoon Grandma asked me what was wrong. I told her everything was just dandy, but I could tell she didn't believe me. Perhaps the small string of sun perch in my hand caused her to doubt. Anyway I told her the whole story and she laughed until she had to sit down. She got a big pleasure out of my foolishness and then went on about her work in the kitchen. She cautioned me not to tell Grandpa about it."

"I didn't tell Grandpa Horton about the incident and he would never have known if Mr. Donohoe hadn't called from school."

"I understand from reliable sources, Mr. Horton, that Roger does not have a good reputation. The grammar school teachers tell me he is an unruly child. I have been warned that he will also cause trouble in my school. So I am calling to warn you and him that I will not tolerate any such behavior as he demonstrated in our school today. I suggest that you impress upon him the importance of staying in class until the 3:30 bell rings. Some of our students saw him leave our campus today. He will be expelled in time, I warn you, if he doesn't abide strictly by our rules. We have to have rules you know."

"According to the agreement between the two men I was given a sound whipping."

"Grandpa, I didn't do anything wrong on purpose, honest I didn't. Grandma'll tell you that. Just ask her. I explained to her how it happened. A girl at school told me a lie. She caused it. Please, grandpa, don't whip me again."

"But my pleas went unheeded."

"Roger, that's the last time you're going to lie to me. I'm going to beat you till the lies are gone for good. You can bring those cock-and-bull stories home to your grandmother if you want to, but you won't get your grandfather to believe them. No siree. You haven't fooled your old grandpa for one minute. Now bend over."

"I saw the futility of trying to reason with granddad so I obliged him and bent over as usual. Then he gave me a severe strapping. When he got through I was sick inside. I don't know how many times he hit me, but I think I would have fainted if he hadn't stopped when he did."

"A deep resentment arose in my heart over such incidents as this. However, I never said anything about it because it didn't do any good. The only one I ever told about my true feelings was the dog. He coudn't tell anybody."

"I was convinced that Grandpa's age kept him from understanding my childishness. He never took my word against others, even when I was right. I felt like a convicted criminal before the trial ever began. He was sole judge and jury as well as prosecuting attorney. He didn't believe grandma either. He accused her of trying to cover up for me."

"No more jokes were pulled on me for awhile after this bitter series of experiences. I had lost confidence in everyone and it got to where obvious truths sounded like lies to me."

"I guess I was around fourteen when I started enjoying church activities more than my school work. Of course I had attended church services regularly every since I went to live with the Hortons, but for some reason I had never been very enthusiastic about it."

"One of the main reasons for my lack of interest was the dull and ineffective teaching methods. My Bible class was unusually dead compared to my classes in school. At school we had pictures on the wall and projects that kept the class feeling as one unit. Then the teachers always had their lessons well prepared too. There was something new nearly every day and we eagerly looked forward to class because of it. But at church, things weren't so bright and cheerful. The rooms were gloomy and bare and the teacher didn't always have his thoughts prepared ahead of time. We students could tell when he didn't and it lowered our morale. We figured if he wasn't interested enough to prepare, then there was no use in our studying at home during the week. So usually when I went to class I just sat there to see what the teacher would forget next."

"I don't know whose business it was to see that qualified persons were teaching, but whoever he was, he was laying down on the job. All we had was the reading of the text, quoting of the memory verse and the answering of the questions at the close of the lesson. That was alright for a beginner, but our teacher had been teaching twelve years and he was no better than when he started. He needed to study some education or something. Maybe his method was good in Daniel Boone's day but it was a long way from the kind of teaching we were getting at the public schools. I knew there must have been some good books on how to teach, but if there were our teacher had never read them. Another thing that caused me to lose respect for my class was our getting out early so much. We were always through before the bell rang. It made me feel that our teacher wasn't as interested in *his* class as other teachers were in theirs."

"Another condition which contributed to my disinterest was my own lack of application. I had never gone to church before coming to Centerville and I missed out on the foundation for church appreciation. My appetite for spiritual things was weak."

"Brother Nellson, the regular preacher for the Church of Christ, was another cause of my disinterest. He was Grandpa's best friend and was as good as gold, but he never realized I was alive. He forgot that he had young people in his audience too. He didn't live in Centerville, but drove over on Sundays from a nearby town. When he was a lad, children were seen and not heard. They were neglected until they were old enough to cause trouble, then they got some notice. My trouble was that he preached over my head. I know I didn't pay as much attention as I should have, but there were reasons for not doing so. If I wasn't understanding what was said my mind wandered off to something else."

"Big words bothered me a lot in Brother Nellson's preaching too. He used a great many of them and never explained what they meant, so I usually got lost somewhere in his vocabulary. It was all adult talk so far as I was concerned. The ideas were very often abstract and illustrations were never used to clarify a point. Preachers just hadn't paid young fellows any mind in *his* generation and we were reaping the results. The things that were said were true and good, but they were too complex for our young minds to grasp. This wasn't young people's talk at all."

"The amount of time I spent in religious activities was also discouraging. The church doors were open three times a week and that was usually all. We met for Bible school and morning worship each Sunday and also at night for the young peoples class and evening worship. Then we met on Wednesday nights for the Mid-week service. But outside of these and the two-week revival each year, these Christian people seldom saw each other."

"Church-going was pure routine with me. We went to every service, but I didn't carry home much for my efforts. Grandpa Horton encouraged me along in my church life, but I didn't respond too well. For one thing I was young and couldn't grasp a lot at a time. But that wasn't all. Everytime Grandpa tried to explain one of those complex sermons I got lost. They quoted too many scriptures without explaining any of them to me. They assumed I would understand, but they didn't know me—I was thick headed."

"It wasn't that I didn't try, because I did try. Nearly every

Sunday morning I was optimistic when I started to service, but too often I came home as ignorant as before. When the lesson began to get too deep for me I resigned myself to youthful ignorance."

"One thing that livened my interest in religious matters was the fun I had at some of the denominational young people's homes. Their Sunday School classes had parties regularly and they invited me quite often. I went as often as I could because I enjoyed associating with groups of young people my age. They had a lot of fun and for the first time I saw that young people could have a good time and be religious too. Somewhere I had picked up the idea that a person had to have his fun first, then he could become a Christian later, but that was wrong. I didn't see these young people doing anything unbecoming the Christian spirit.

"During the summer months the denominational church families took great pains to keep their young people together enjoying themselves. I could tell that what they were doing was wholesome and would be good for the young people where I attended church, but we didn't have anything provided for us."

"Grandpa and Grandma Horton didn't like my going to these denominational class parties, but there was little they could say as long as they didn't do wrong things. They had no argument against it. They hadn't provided me with something better to do, so I convinced them to let me keep going. I didn't care what church the young people belonged to; all I was interested in was the association and the ice cream and lemonade."

"These parties outside the church did not always limit themselves to the type of entertainment my folks could approve of however. One of them began to give ballroom dances. The parents ran out of things for their young folks to do, so they turned to dancing as a substitute. I was skeptical from the first and never thought that dancing should be a part of a church group's recreational activities, but I soon got used to it. There wasn't any other group entertaining in town so I had little choice."

"When the Horton's learned of these dances they insisted that I stop going to the parties. I thought this was unfair. They wanted me to stop doing bad, but they didn't offer me anything good in its place. I resented their short-sighted attitude. I finally

61

took the position that dancing was alright so long as adult chaperones were present, but this was only my defense for my unwise desire to go with the crowd no matter what they did."

"I had never discussed the right and wrong of dancing with anyone. I just had the impression that church folk were against it. I didn't know why they were against it."

"We had a real knock down and drag out when the Hortons found out I kept going to the denominational parties where the dancing was encouraged. I lied to them about my whereabouts and for a long time they didn't catch up with me. This caused quite a stir among the people at the church too. Grandpa was an elder there and my actions were bad for him. However, some members of the congregation took the hint and began to provide their children with more home activities. This was in self-defense, but that was better than nothing. This group was only a small minority, but at least it was a start. Now what they needed was a leader who knew something about the needs of adolescent young people. He needed to stir the parents up until they realized that their young people were going to have fun. We preferred doing *good* things, but if they weren't provided we'd settle for bad things. Sometimes we didn't have much choice."

"Until now I only obeyed my grandparents half-heartedly, but I did obey. But their command to quit the parties was too much. I refused to quit. This was the only fun I had and I was determined to keep it up no matter what it cost me."

"It wasn't that I liked to dance, because I didn't know how. But I did enjoy association. It was a relief from my loneliness and depressed feeling. As long as I didn't actually dance I didn't feel guilty, but I never thought of my presence there amounting to my consent."

"A few months after my flareup with my grandparents there was a change made at the church. Brother Nellson resigned his work because he was too old to continue driving the forty miles from his home each Sunday. His doctors had advised him to give up his work because of his high blood pressure. His resignation interrupted our usual routine for awhile, but it didn't seriously hurt the work. The elders spoke in turns while the congregation was looking for a new preacher."

62

"Finally, after three months of searching, the elders, with Brother Nellson's help, secured a new preacher for the Centerville church. He was a young man from a good Christian family. He had finished his schooling and was working at a secular job and doing part-time preaching for a small congregation in Virginia. Brother Nellson, his life-time friend, persuaded him to take up the ministry full time and go to Centerville. When the church heard that he had accepted their invitation to work with them, they anxiously awaited his arrival."

"I didn't let on that the new preacher's coming meant anything to me. I supposed he would preach over my head too, so his coming didn't make me any difference."

"When the new preacher arrived he was shown through the church building and then entertained at a dinner with all the elders and deacons and their wives present. I didn't see him until the next day."

"Brother Ainsworth came to Centerville one Saturday morning and was introduced to the congregation the next day at services. \He was blond haired and short, about 5' 8" tall. He had blue eyes and a very prominent chin. It was easy to tell that he was a man of strong conviction. I could tell it by the set of his jaw."

"I'll have to admit that I was pleased that Brother Ainsworth was given our boys class to teach. Our other teacher had been transferred to another town by his company. Though I was pleased I didn't let on that I was. I told the other boys I didn't care who taught our class."

"I'll never forget Brother Ainsworth's first sermon. He spoke on 'A Closer Walk With Christ.' I had never heard many preachers so I wasn't able to judge very well, but I liked his simple preaching. In his sermon he analyzed the lives of several people who walked with Jesus. He explained how these weak and unstable men, like Peter, became pillars in the church. Then he showed us how we could walk closer to Christ too."

"The new preacher, with his plain and powerful approach caught me off guard. Much to my surprise I understood nearly everything that was said. When he used a big word he defined it or explained its use. When he taught an abstract principle he illustrated it by some Bible story or an example from everyday life. His manner of presenting the lesson was so simple that I often felt I could do as well—maybe better. But when I tried making talks in my class I found out how hard it was to make things clear and simple. At first I was interested in *how* he delivered his sermons, but before long I became so interested in what was said that I forgot all else."

"I remember too, that I didn't go over to Charlie's house after dinner that Sunday, as was my custom. Instead, I stayed in my room and thought about the things I had heard that morning. I thought it was strange that one sermon should affect me so, but it had a grip on me and wouldn't let go of my mind."

"Brother Ainsworth was anxious to make his position about the Christian's responsibilities clear. The main point in his lesson had been that every person is expected to take a stand for Christ."

"My good friends, Jesus did not leave us to choose our way of life. Instead He said, 'He that is not with me is against me; and he that gathereth not with me scattereth abroad.' Now you will note that He did not mention a middle group here. We are either for Christ or we are against Him. He drew a line then didn't he? Sinners are on one side and Christians on the other. Those who walk close to His side are for Him and those who lag behind are scattered abroad. Its all or none with Him. He wants us hot or cold, but never lukewarm. God despises lukewarm people. They never take a stand. They're cowards in the spirit. Every person in this audience is either for Christ or against Him—today!"

"I remember well these remarks by the preacher. They cut deep into my heart and exposed me as a sinner. I hadn't taken a stand for Christ. Because I was lukewarm I had never made a decision in His favor. Somehow I had never thought about the preaching applying to me. I had listened to it month after month and looked around at other sinners. But now I was seeing the real sinner—Roger Scott. It hurt my pride some to admit that I wasn't strong enough or wise enough to run my own life, but it was true. I was weak and ignorant. When Brother Ainsworth pounded the pulpit and said 'You are either for or against Christ—today' he was looking straight at me, or at least I felt that he was.

Later he told me he wasn't looking at anyone in particular, so I misjudged him."

"Brother Ainsworth was different. He could be shooting fire from his eyes one minute as he denounced sin and calming the audience the next minute with an expression of love and concern which no one could mistake. Throughout his preaching the audience was aware that he was opposed to everything that was devilish and for everything that was good. He preached hard at times as he exposed current trends which were harmful to the lives of the Christians in Centerville. He asked the women and young girls if they would walk down the street with Christ in their shorts and halters. This really made them squirm. Then he asked them why they dressed indecently like this and expected Christian men to want to be seen with them. He also stunned some of the boys present when he told them how foul their cursing really was. He usually didn't leave anyone out. There was something helpful in each sermon for all. He closed his sermon by reminding the audience of God's wrath."

"If you cannot be touched by the goodness and longsuffering of God then perhaps the severity of God will stir your sleeping soul. The Lord has reserved a burning Hell for those who disobey his Will. In Revelation 20:15 the Apostle John called Hell a 'lake of fire.' In Revelation 14:11 He told us that 'the smoke of the tormented ascended up forever and forever and they had no rest day or night.' Just remember, God will send His goodness upon those who love Him and His wrath upon those who wilfully disobey Him. It is your choice, not His; not mine! You must make up your own mind. Make your decision for Christ today while we stand and encourage you to do so by the singing of this song."

"This kind of straight preaching sure got me to thinking. It proved which side of the fence I was on. Though I had never thought of it this way, it showed me I had been taking Christ for granted. I had been expecting Him to save me and bless my life, but I hadn't done anything for Him—not even obey the gospel. That scripture the preacher quoted, 'work out your own salvation with fear and trembling' made me feel guilty. I don't know what I must have been thinking, but until now I had never paid the idea of salvation much mind. Before this I had never felt like a very big sinner; I didn't drink or smoke, or cuss, or steal or gamble or do any of those things. That's why I thought I was a pretty good person. But now I realized I wasn't so good after all. I was in danger."

"There was preaching at the church house again that night. The subject this time was 'The New Testament Salvation.' The sermon was mostly a review of the conversions in the book of Acts. He said that sinners became Christians the same way in every case according to this book."

"You see, my friends, the Lord has not left us to work out our own salvation without some guide. That's why we have the book of Acts. One case after the other illustrates the Lord's way of converting sinners into faithful disciples. Why the duplication? So no man can miss it. When the Lord gives over a half-dozen instances of people becoming Christians, and all are converted the same way, then we conclude that we have sufficient evidence to guide us to remission of sins today. Take Acts 2:38 for instance. Peter was speaking to a believing audience. They confessed their faith with the question 'Men and brethren, what shall we do?' So whatever Peter told them to do was what they lacked yet in obeying the gospel completely. So he told them to 'Repent and be baptized, everyone of you, in the name of the Lord Jesus Christ, and ye shall receive the gift of the Holy Spirit.' Three thousand sin-stricken Jews obeyed the gospel at that time."

"Now to the eighth chapter of Acts and the cases of the Samaritans, Simon and the Ethiopian eunuch. In each case, these folks were lost in sin. They became concerned about their condition and sought help also. After hearing the gospel they expressed their faith and were baptized for the remission of sins. You will note that they were doing nothing more than obeying the will of Christ. He said in Mark 16:16 'He that believeth and is baptized shall be saved . . . .'"

"Then to continue with our line of thought we notice the 9th, 10th and 16th chapters of Acts. In these chapters Saul, Cornelius, Lydia, and the Philippian Jailer were also saved by believing and being baptized. Their faith, in every case, was proved by their repentance and public confession of their desire to obey Christ.

This same truth is also evident in the 18th and 19th chapters."

"Now let me summarize the thought of this lesson. Here are nine cases of conversion in which sinners, once convicted of guilt, turned to the Lord in true faith and obeyed the gospel for the remission of their sins. Once baptized they were newborn children of God and members of the church. Now let me ask each of you a vital question. Are you a Christian? If not, why not? Have you ever asked yourself the question? And did you give yourself an honest answer? Now ask yourself this. Would your answer be pleasing to God? If not, why not reconsider this important matter tonight and make your decision in favor of Christ. We will now stand and sing our invitation song with the prayer that you will surrender your life to Jesus. If you will, you will enjoy the New Testament salvation."

"There was little question about it. Brother Ainsworth's sermons were aimed directly at the hearts of sinners, and he was reaching mine. This surprised me somewhat, because I had always thought religion was for big folks and that I would have to be grown before I understood the Bible, but I found out different. The preacher had announced in his first sermon that he would try to present the truth so that every person in the audience could understand it, if at all possible. He said his aim in preaching was to make the truth so plain that the untaught and the young could understand it. He said if they grasped Christ's teachings then he would not worry about the higher educated and older folks.

"My spare time the following week was spent in reading and rereading the book of Acts. This sudden interest in the Bible was puzzling to me as well as my grandparents. However, they didn't say anything. I guess they believed in letting well enough alone. But I didn't let the matter drop so easily. I wondered myself why I was so concerned about my soul now, whereas before it didn't bother me. Maybe I just understood more or else I was getting old enough to understand better."

"After thinking the matter over many hours I felt compelled to settle the matter of my soul's salvation once and for all. I was already two or three years older than most of the young people were when they obeyed Christ. They had already enjoyed freedom from the guilt of sin and the peace of mind which went with it, but I was still an alien sinner. Somehow I had never clearly realized what I had been missing, but I was seeing now. Peace of mind—that had been my quest all the time, but I knew I couldn't have it while my conscience kept telling me I was against Christ. Now I knew that I couldn't expect freedom from sin. I had to do something so God's grace could be granted me. This realization of my need to get closer to God weighed heavily on my heart, but I was afraid. I knew that when I became a Christian I would have to go all the way. He wouldn't take anyone halfway. He had already said He didn't want any lukewarm or half-hearted children. I wasn't sure whether I could go all the way with Him. I wasn't positive I wanted to. Then I remembered that after I became a Christian I would have to walk a straighter path than I had been. I thought that was quite an order for a boy of my age. So the arguments in my mind went on. I didn't want to get tied down to the church and yet I didn't want to go on living without Christ and the hope of eternal life either. Like the preacher said, no one knows when he's going to the grave so he ought to be ready at all times. I was certain of one thing. I wanted above all to avoid the risk of spending eternity in Hell after I died."

The Hortons were dumbfounded over Roger's quiet and meditative conduct through this period of his life. They held their breath for fear the spell would soon be broken and their old antagonisms would crop up again. Though they were both very puzzled about this new conduct neither of them suspected the real cause of it.

"Night after night I lay awake past midnight looking into the limitless sky, wondering where God was. I knew He was up there somewhere but I couldn't imagine just what He must be like. I had been told that He was the great Spirit up there somewhere beyond the vision of the mortal eye, but I still wondered. No, I did more than that. *I believed.* Somehow I felt closer to God now that my thoughts were on a loftier plain and I liked the experience. It may me feel good and clean inside. My stubborn will was at last giving in and I was becoming more reconciled to the decision I was about to make. I considered and reconsidered the cost of discipleship and the more I thought about the blessings I would get the more I was persuaded to accept them—regardless of cost. I continued to pray after this, but my prayers were different now. I no longer asked for personal things or even for the Lord to save me. I knew now that I had no right to ask those things of Him until I obeyed His will. Then I could ask for anything that was good and proper. I had about made up my mind to become a Christian the next Sunday. I thought that would be what Christ wanted me to do."

"Along with my communion with God I enjoyed another blessing. My terrible agony of feeling lonely and unwanted was going away. I felt that if God would love me then it didn't matter about anyone else. I felt a nearness to Christ now and I was confident that He would be my friend."

"I took a lot more interest in the Bible school class the next Sunday. The young preacher knew what we young people liked to study, so he picked out the points that would especially apply to our everyday lives. That was what we were most interested in. Too, he let us do a lot of the talking. He got the subject started and then everyone who wanted to could speak. That made us all feel that the class was part ours. We were encouraged to ask questions, and we asked plenty of them, and very often we were asked to explain something in the lesson, which we tried to do. This made us feel very important. We liked our class now."

"Following the Bible class came the worship service in the auditorium. We had the usual songs and prayer and then the Lord's Supper was served as it was every Sunday. Then the preacher began his sermon. I was nervous all morning and my tension grew when the end of his lesson came closer. By the time the invitation song was started I was shaking all over, though I tried to conceal it by moving my arms around a little."

"For others in the audience the singing and praying and preaching had been about as usual, but not for me. I was plenty scared, but I remembered everything about the service. And when the invitation was extended I was ready. I let them sing one stanza and then I forced my left foot out into the aisle. It wasn't any trouble after that since my right foot *had* to follow. I

69

walked down the aisle to the front and Brother Ainsworth smiled at me as he took me by the hand and had me stand close to him. I told him I wanted to become a Christian so he heard my confession immediately."

"Roger Scott, do you believe with all your heart that Jesus is the Christ, the Son of the living God?"

"I do."

"This young man has just confessed the name of his Lord and Savior, the Christ. This is a fine step in his life and he is to be highly commended for it. This is also the decision the Lord expects *every* young boy and girl to make when they come to realize their need of a Savior. It was Jesus himself who said 'Whosoever therefore shall confess me before men, him will I confess before my Father who is in Heaven.' So Roger, your name is now being confessed to God the Father in Heaven."

"I was led into one of the side classrooms where I changed clothes and got ready to be baptized. The congregation sang two songs while we were changing. Both songs were my favorites. The first one was 'What A Friend We Have In Jesus' and the other was 'O Happy Day.'"

The preacher and Roger went into the baptistry together. Once standing in the water the preacher raised his right hand and said, "And now by the authority of our Lord and Savior, Jesus Christ, I baptize you in the name of the Father, and of the Son, and of the Holy Spirit for the remission of your sins. Amen." Then the preacher laid Roger back in the water until his whole body was well submerged. This represented his death to past sins and the burial of that old man of sin. Then the preacher raised him up out of the water. This was his resurrection from the death of the sinful man. Now he was in Christ and was a new creature spiritually. He had received forgiveness of sins and became a child of God and a member of the church at the same time.

"A great many things improved in my life after my conversion. I felt much better and had a brighter outlook on life. I decided everyone wasn't against me after all. At least their eagerness to help me now didn't seem to indicate opposition to me. But the great relief to me was the goal in life I had achieved. My mission

70

in life now was to uphold the standard of Christ and march fearlessly in his spiritual army. I was determined to hold His banner high."

"For a long time after my conversion I felt no fears or worries of any kind. I was willing to live and let the world get along as best it could. I was happier too when the young people at the church acted friendlier to me and tried to include me into their activities more. My outlook toward school and my homelife was better too. I wanted to cooperate more and make others happy, as well as be happy myself. I even respected my grandfather's advice and counseled with him at times. My school grades rose again and my teachers were pleased with my improvement and told me so."

"By the time I was sixteen I had grown up physically and entered my junior year in high school. And since I was better adjusted in every way I began to take more interest in the activities at the school. I noticed that other young people were going lots of places and having lots of fun that I hadn't missed before. But now I wanted to go with them. I wanted to laugh like they did and go out of town with them and stay up late on week ends. And above all I wanted to join one of the school clubs. In our town if a fellow didn't belong to one of the high school social clubs he just wasn't anybody. When I was invited I joined the No-name Club. This was a non-official group of juniors and seniors who hadn't been invited into the other clubs and since I hadn't been invited by any others, I accepted their invitation gladly."

"As the months went by it became the rule rather than the exception for a horn to blow in front of our house several nights a week. The folks didn't like my going out so much on school nights, but I out-argued them on it. By now I was like nearly all the other young people in Centerville. I was always ready to go someplace and hoped I didn't have to stay still over a minute at a time."

"I must have gotten pretty silly at this time too. Grandma Horton thought I was getting it from the crowd I was running with, but that wasn't altogether the truth. I just felt real good and found a lot to giggle about. Everything seemed funny to me for some reason. I'll never know how the Horton's put up with me, but somehow they lived through it."

"All the gang thought about was sports, sports and more sports. That's all we talked about when we were together. We went to all the ball games at the school and also made the out-of-town games. At first I went to the games with the Club, not because I understood the sports, but because it was somewhere to go and someone to go with. This was my first chance to really have friends and I was very proud of myself."

"I didn't know much about the No-name Club when I went into it and I didn't pay it much mind as they began to count me in on all their activities. They were weaving me into *their* pattern of activities and for the longest I thought it was the normal adolescent behavior at Centerville High. The changes came in me so gradually that I didn't suspect them. But I found out later that this was all a part of their plan. The charter members of the club were worldly-wise for their age and they knew a thing or two about modern psychology."

"Without my suspicions being aroused I began to feel a strong loyalty to my Club. I felt so strong about it in time that I was ready to go anywhere with them at any time—no questions asked. I'm sure some of my church friends noticed my loss of restraint, but they were afraid to challenge me on the matter. I guess its best they didn't because I wasn't in any frame of mind to hear anything against my buddies in the Club."

Besides making all the ball games, the No-name club always attended the after-the-games dances in the high school gym. And as usual Roger went along for the ride.

"I couldn't dance a step when I joined the gang. As a matter of fact it embarrassed me to be seen there, but I thought I had to stay with my Club. I knew the church people didn't approve of the dances, but I thought few of them would ever know whether I was there or not. Though I worried about this matter awhile at first, I soon got used to it and finally forgot about it entirely. I was determined to have a lot of fun like all the other kids in town and I wasn't too concerned about what it was or who it was with."

"There was an incident on a Friday night which did shake me a great deal. It even made me reconsider my views on the high

72

school dances. I was standing over by the wall as usual watching the others dance and I noticed Jay Robinson. He was one of the young people's leaders in a denomination in town. I had heard him make several serious religious talks and knew he had the reputation of being a stable thinker. But now he was out on the floor with a girl showing off some kind of new dance and was making a spectacle of himself. I didn't get it. A few days before he was making a very serious talk in the assembly about keeping our heads as young people in the community, and now he was out on the dance floor going wild. After this I never listened to him seriously."

"A few of my own close friends finally approached me about going to the dances. They contended that I would eventually take up the activity myself and be just as bad as the rest of them about going to the highway taverns and dance halls. But I denied everything and explained that I didn't participate, I just watched and that was all I would ever do."

"Later I had to take my strong words back. The girls kept asking me and teasing me about being afraid to dance until I had to prove to them that I wasn't. Then after I started trying to learn I liked it and got real interested. They were patient with me and before long I was doing pretty good at it. And the more I thought of the girls I could meet this way the better I liked my decision to start it."

"One day Brother Ainsworth met me on the sidewalk in town and told me he would like to speak with me a few minutes at his office. I knew what he wanted. I had already argued the matter out with my folks and knew I would have to debate the issue with the preacher sooner or later. This was sooner, but I agreed to the meeting anyway."

"Grandma and Grandpa Horton had forcefully told me of their objections to my disobedience in frequenting the dances. And though I didn't heed their advice I didn't forget their words."

"Son, your grandmother and me don't want to deprive you of anything that's good. We just don't want you to hurt yourself—and us too for that matter. As an elder of the church I don't look so good to the town with my grandson staying out until all hours of the night dancing and running around with that No-nothing

Club or whatever you call it. And the church will be hurt too, son. Think of them. Folks will start saying 'if that's the way those Church of Christ folks do, we don't want any part of them. They do wrong and try to say its right.' Now don't you see my point? You'll hurt yourself, us, the church and the name of the Lord. You told Him you'd do better, but are you doing it?"

"Grandpa tried demanding obedience from me at first, but he soon took to reasoning with me. I was close to six feet tall now and weighed about 160 pounds so it was hard for him to discipline me like he used to. And I was strong now too. I wished a time or two that he would try to whip me again. I was irritated enough to fight him. Then I would have had something to brag to the Club about."

"I met the preacher at the appointed place and time for our talk. We met in one of the classrooms which was used also for his office. I hadn't had much to do with preachers before so I was awkward at the beginning. I didn't know how to act but I soon learned that they were human like everyone else and wanted to be considered as such."

"The preacher wasn't long in showing me that ministers can be very nice as well as firm. His congenial smile told me right off that no matter how much we differed we weren't going to argue or get mad at one another. That relieved me a lot."

"Roger, I haven't called you here to take advantage of you or abuse you about your problems. You've got enough worries without me adding any to them. But I do believe you need help before you get into your problem any deeper. I called you here to offer to help you. You see, I'm a little older than you and know something of what you're going through. If you keep going as you are I see dark days ahead. I don't say we can solve everything, but I do think we can help you avoid a lot of trouble. I can see things and mention them to you in hopes that you will look ahead to the eventual results. You need to weigh both sides of every question and decide which will bring you happiness and which will harm you. Now you must choose. Either you can make all of your own decisions or you can let me or someone else who is interested in your affairs help you. Now what do you say? Are you willing for me to discuss these matters

74

with you? I can help you avoid an awful lot of pitfalls. And don't believe everything some people tell you about preachers. They aren't stuff-shirts at all, as a rule. They're people, like you, and they've dedicated their lives to help people. That's what they're for. So you see I'm not trying to butt into your business I'm trying to discharge a responsibility I feel very keenly."

"I told the preacher I didn't mind talking to him, or anybody else. I told him my life was an open book and anyone could read it that wanted to. But that was the trouble. Brother Ainsworth had read a coming chapter of my life and he didn't like it. He was afraid for my future happiness."

"I acted brave, but I was really unnerved. The preacher acted like he knew what he was talking about. Too, he had been right about everything else he told me, so I felt that I should listen to him now."

"Brother Ainsworth saw that I was willing to listen so we began to talk. He went right to the point and he didn't compromise any truth as he told me the kind of recreation a young Christian should participate in and the kinds of people he should associate with."

CHAPTER 5

AFTER THE DANCE

Roger didn't know how long he had been lying there in his cell thinking back over his past. Sometimes he felt that time was speeding by, but at other times he hardly thought it was passing at all. Very soft sounds were coming from the jury room so it appeared that the jurymen were either coming to some agreement or were becoming weary.

Roger shook his head in regret as he remembered the excellent advice the preacher had given him about his dancing. He regretted that he had not listened to him.

●

"I'm not going to spare many words with you Roger, I have plenty of evidence to back up my position about your dancing. But let me reason with you a little before I bring up my evidence. Maybe I won't have to convince you through other's mistakes. Now I know its hard for a young man like you to take advice from others at this time. You think you have a lot at stake, and maybe you do. Maybe you have more at stake than you realize. I hope you haven't closed your mind on the subject because there's quite a lot for you to consider on the other side of the question."

"I wasn't really listening to Brother Ainsworth. I was too prejudiced against anybody who would take my fun away from me. This was the first group that ever took to me and I thought a lot of their friendship. I'm sure now that I wasn't capable of reasoning with the preacher at all. My mind was made up and I was afraid if I listened to anyone too much I would want to quit the gang—that was what I didn't want to happen."

The young preacher sensed immediately that Roger was act-

76

ing selfishly rather than reasoning intelligently. He felt that he couldn't tell the boy anything. He would just have to find out for himself.

"So you take the position that dancing is just good, clean exercise. Well I've heard that one before. But do you know that I have yet to find one person who could prove it. Besides there are too many other ways to get wholesome exercise. Ways which are above reproach. Now what do you say we try an experiment. If it works then you gain the right to attend all the dances you want to. But if you lose then you will be much better off to learn that dancing is more than just exercise. I'm suggesting that there is some lust involved. Oh, I know a lot of young people never dream of getting involved in anything where lust is concerned, but they do nonetheless. They just don't realize why they like to dance. You say its for the exercise. I say it is for the gratification of a developing urge within young people. They aren't emotionally mature, that's true, but they are maturing and there's a physical satisfaction enjoyed when a boy holds a girl's body that close to his. Underneath it all, whether you're willing to admit it or not, there is the craving for the satisfaction of one of the human drives. And God doesn't want that sex urge to be stimulated in this or any other such manner. It invariably produces unwise thoughts which in turn foster a growing lust which, if not properly checked, ends in either sin in heart or body."

"I was getting the point, alright, but I didn't like it. I hadn't begun dancing for any such reason as this. I just wasn't guilty! I went to the dances to be with the other kids, that's all. But then I'll have to admit too that I got to enjoying dancing with the girls. I never thought about figuring out why."

"Now here's my proposition," the preacher continued. "I'll give two dances for your crowd if you think they'll come."

"Oh, they'll be there alright. They'll go to any dance anywhere. They'd even go to one you put on, that is if you'd also have something to eat."

"Fine! Now here's what I'll do. I'll give two dances next week. Say, one on Thursday night and one Friday night. How does that sound?"

"That sounds great! Boy, won't they be surprised when they hear that they've been invited to a dance sponsored by you. That'll knock their hats off."

"Whoa, there! I'm not through. Here's the rest. Since you say your dancing is just for the exercise, I'll give one for the girls on Thursday night and another dance for the boys the next night. Then they can get their exercise to their heart's content."

"Aw, that's no bargain at all! That's cheap. You know they won't do anything like that. That's the silliest thing I ever heard of. Why they'd laugh us both out of town if I put it up to them that way. Look here, you knew they wouldn't accept a deal like that. That's the reason you offered to give the dances in the first place. You knew they wouldn't take you up on it. That's not being fair."

"To the contrary, Roger, I'm being consistent with your reasoning. Can't you see that? If they dance just for the fun of it, and that fun is just the exercise they get out of it, then they'll be glad to accept my offer. But on the other hand, if they don't like my offer you can well see that it involves more than just exercise. Maybe you do dance just for the exercise. But they don't! And I really doubt that you do. I don't honestly believe you understand what you're doing or why. My point is this. Those boys and girls get together because there's something of a thrill in it for them. Now I'm saying that the thrill mentioned is the beginning of the gratification of lust. It's insignificant at first, but as those boys and girls age and mature emotionally they find this passion, or lust if you want to call it that, growing also. Such familiarity between young men and women was never a part of God's scheme of things. It fosters harmful thoughts and has led to shame and disgrace in some instances. Son, I'm not trying to take anything away from you that's good. I'm just trying to spare you the inevitable problems which will be yours if you stay with this crowd you're running with. They call themselves the No-name Club. Why? They don't want to be identified with anything that's good. The other clubs have names taken from one source or the other, but your bunch wants to be so secretive that they don't even want a name."

"We gotta do something! We can't sit around every night and

twiddle our thumbs. We gotta have our fun while we can. There's nothing wrong with my gang and we like the name too. They're alright."

"Look, Roger, most people are very much alike. Your crowd doesn't mix with the majority of the students at the school and you know it. They don't want good clean fun. I have reason to suspect that your No-name Club is nothing but a bunch of kids who think its smart to smoke and drink and cuss."

"Well if they did, you wouldn't have nothing to say about it. What have you all done to give us something interesting to do? Ask Grandpa Horton, he won't even let me start a woodshop of my own. He won't let me do anything I want to do. So what do I do? I stay away from home all I can and tend to my own business. I don't hurt nobody and I don't want nobody nosing into my business either."

"I'm really sorry to hear you talk that way, son. Now you sound like those punks you chum around with. You're not their type. Now why don't you get away from them while the getting's good? Oh, I'll admit there isn't much being provided you young people at the church to do, but we can change that. It will take time, but I think we can arouse the parents to their obligation in this matter in time; but Roger you need to be patient. If you will, we should have a very interesting setup before too long. That bunch you're with right now just isn't the kind a Christian young boy should be around. They're up to no good."

" 'That's a lie,' I told him. 'I guess I run around with them. They don't do all those things you accuse them of. That's what's wrong with so many of you adults now. You're always talking about stuff you don't know anything about."

"Then what do you say we try another experiment? This will show you what dancing and associating with that crowd will do to your Christian influence. As a matter of fact, I dare you to try it. I doubt that you're brave enough."

"I'm brave enough to do anything you can dream up. Just give me the details and I'll show you."

"Then Brother Ainsworth told me his plan. Of course, I agreed to it. What else could I do? I had already bragged about what all I could do. We shook hands and I left the meeting determined to show that preacher a thing or two."

The following Friday night found Roger at the high school gym—dancing as usual. After a half dozen numbers had been played on the juke box he got up enough courage to try out the experiment. Now he was to make his report on Monday.

"Brother Ainsworth was in his office Monday afternoon like he said he would be. I sure hated to go in there, but I had made a promise and I don't like to go back on my promises."

"Well, Roger, how did you come out last Friday night? Did you talk to any of the girls about becoming a Christian? You remember that was the problem. I said you couldn't be an influence for Christ around such people as that and in such a place as that. You said you could. Now I want to know which of us was right. I'm not trying to embarrass you, I just want to find out your results."

"But I was embarrassed. And I finally found enough breath to speak."

"Then tell me all about it and don't spare the details. I'm anxious to know how you came out."

"It didn't work out good at all. Everything happened about like you said it would."

"Is that so?" said the preacher. "Then tell me all about it."

"It just didn't work out, that's all. I tried it and it didn't work. That's all there is to tell."

"No, no, Roger. I want the details. I want to know what the girls said. Now come on and tell me. I'm your friend and I'm trying to understand you and help you."

"Alright, I'll tell you. I didn't talk to but one girl about it. And after I finished with her I didn't want to talk to anyone else. That one was humiliating enough."

"Yes, go on. Tell me what you two said. I may want this information for future reference. Of course I'll not use names and places, but I would very much like to know what words were exchanged."

"Something was wrong. The atmosphere wasn't right or something. Maybe it was the record they were playing. Anyway, I was dancing with Lula Anderson. I thought she was probably the best girl there. She used to attend all the Sunday school class parties I went to, so I got the impression that she must have been pretty religious. I just knew she would agree with me. But when I asked her if she was a faithful Christian you should have seen her face. She told me she wasn't and didn't intend to be until she had her fun. And when she asked me the same question I blushed for five minutes. That wasn't the place to discuss things like that. I felt odd in even bringing up the subject. She didn't talk very nice to me either."

"Roger, if you're a Christian what are you doing here? You know this is no place for a Christian young person. What will the other girls think of you? Its a good thing they don't know it because if they did they might think you were spying on us. You'd better not tell anybody else. What are you trying to do, throw a wet blanket on our fun?"

"And with that Lula walked off and left me. She didn't want to be around me after she found out I claimed to be a faithful Christian. What was the matter with her? She puzzled me!"

"Then you see my reasons for opposing such activity don't you Roger? That is not the place for a Christian young person to frequent. Nor are those the kind of young people the Lord would want you around. Remember he said 'Evil companionship corrupts good morals.' And as I've explained before, the familiarity involved is everything but wholesome. Don't you see you can't be a faithful Christian and be a faithful member of that crowd at the same time? You're trying to serve two masters, and it won't work. Sooner or later you'll be forced to make a choice. I pray you'll make the right one."

"You talk like dancing is the only sin in the world. What about the other ones? And what about the other kids in the church here too, they're not angels. Why don't you call them in and bawl them out?"

"Let's keep the record straight, Roger. I'm not bawling you out and dancing isn't the only sin in the world. Certainly it isn't, but that's going to prove the starting point of your troubles. Keep away from trouble and trouble will keep away from you. But you're diving headlong into it, so you can't expect anything but harm to come to you. And as for the other young people in this congregation, they have their troubles too, just like you. They aren't all exactly like yours, but they all have some. As a matter of fact two or three of them have had me discuss their problems with them. Two of them invited me into their homes to discuss the matter with them and their parents. The other one talked with me by phone. Now let me try to summarize what I've been trying to get across to you. First, you get with this outcast gang or club as they call it. Then you start going to dances with them. They're bad medicine. They put you in bad company and tempt you to do wrong things. And don't forget that the usual companions with dancing are drinking, smoking and gambling. Those other things come along sooner or later down the line."

"You still haven't convinced me. I think its all a lot of fun."

"It may be to you now, son, but what about later? Take for instance the reports by nationally known doctors and lawyers and judges. Look at the crime records. The police chiefs and judges say that 80% of all the women in this country who get in trouble with the law started at the dance. Or you could ask the F. B. I. for their records. They'd also tell you that thousands of young women each year admit that they were influenced to throw away their lives in sex crimes and it all began with the wrong kind of people at dances. So you see, it isn't just the dance itself that's wrong. Its everything that goes with it and follows after it."

"But our high school dances don't have any drinking and gambling with them. There's just a bunch of young people who like to be together and enjoy themselves each Friday night. That's all."

"But how many of those young people who learned to dance will stop dancing when their high school days are over? And how many of those youngsters will be strong enough to withstand the drinking and gambling which goes on in those beer halls and dance halls out on the highway? Now suppose, because you go to these dances some other boy, say William Hines, starts going. You're strong enough to stop when you graduate from high school, but he isn't. He's weak and you influenced him. Then he goes to these road houses frequently and finally is killed at one of them in a drunken brawl. You would be partly responsible wouldn't you? You got him started! If it hadn't been for your dancing he never would have died. Now don't say this couldn't happen because it can. As a matter of fact William's parents are having a time with him about this subject now. He says he ought to be allowed to go if you do. However, I think we've just about convinced him of the seriousness of his request."

"I gotta go now. I think I understand everything better. Thanks for the talk."

"One more thing, Roger. Whatever decision you make, I want you to feel free to talk with me about it. We understand each other now and there's no reason why we can't go on being friends. I'm ready to help you if you get in trouble. So call me when you need me—and I'm afraid you will."

"I didn't like the preacher's suggestion that I was headed for trouble at all. I thought I knew what I was doing and I wasn't afraid of getting into any serious difficulty. However, the next few days were disagreeable ones. One minute I decided to throw the whole gang overboard and get me some new friends. But the next minute I would get cold feet. I wasn't sure I could get any more friends. I had heard that once a fellow got in the No-name Club he couldn't run around with any of the other groups."

The No-name Club learned about Roger's conference with Brother Ainsworth through round-about means. For one thing it was written all over his face the next few days at school. Roger wasn't friendly and carefree as before.

"The club felt like they were in a crisis I guess. Anyway, they had some conferences of their own to discuss my case. They were afraid if anyone dropped out of the dances that others might follow suit and the whole thing would fold up. I knew that only about a sixth of the students ever went to the dances, but I didn't think my quitting would stop any others."

The internal conflict in Roger's heart went on for several days more.

"I wanted the gang's approval as well as their association, but I didn't like the way my conscience hurt me. It was awfully hard for me to make up my mind. Finally I decided to quit. I didn't go the next Friday night. And I paid for it too! The next week was a hard one. The members of the club gave me the cold shoulder and snubbed me every time they saw me. I had no one else to turn to, so here I was out in the cold again—right back where I started."

The No-name Club members were cunning kids. They increased the pressure on Roger at every opportunity. And if these measures had failed they planned to start tales on him around the school and completely ruin his influence. They planned to set him up as an example of what would happen to any other deserters from their ranks.

"I was dealing with some ruthless minds but didn't know it at the time. I didn't approve of their cursing and general loose behavior, but I didn't suspect just how low the club really was. They put the pressure on me, alright, and it worked. I just couldn't take the embarrassment. I felt like I had to conform. I guess I didn't have the moral fiber at the time to resist."

The Club received Roger back with great jubilation. They had won out over the preacher's influence and they were gloating about it.

"They had taken my will away from me is what it amounted to. I knew it at the time, but I wasn't strong enough to do anything about it. As long as I went along quietly I got along with them fine. After this they sorta made me their goat and their yes-man, but I knew I had to do these things in order to get along with them."

A few weeks later the Club felt very confident of their hold over Roger so they decided to let him go a step further in their organization. Until now he had never been allowed to stay out with them past midnight, but now they expected him to stay with them later.

"It was about two weeks later that I really got to know my gang. As usual I went driving with them after the dance. This night there were three carloads. This was to be my initiation night so I was a little excited. Some of the football boys were along and they were all bragging about who was the strongest and the toughest. Then they got out their bottles of wine and tried to show how tough they were by outdrinking each other. I could tell it was burning their throats but they didn't let on that it was. The girls squeeled with glee and admiration as the boys took turns at the bottle. And occasionally the girls took a nip too just to show they were regular fellows. All this behavior shocked me at first. I didn't know they drank and carried on like this. Probably that was because they hadn't trusted me before and didn't do these things in front of me. But now they didn't care."

The three cars followed the leader from one roadhouse to the other. Usually they raced each other down the highway after the traffic let up.

"Three of the boys soon got a little groggy and they didn't know much that happened the rest of the ride. When I was handed the bottle I didn't want it, but they said this was my initiation into the secret order. I didn't like either the smell or the taste of the whiskey they gave me. I asked if I couldn't have one of the bottles of wine, but they turned me down. I drank as little as I could but it burned all the way down. By now over half the couples in our group were drunk. The revelry increased and some of the girls acted downright wild. Then came the real surprise. Lile, one of the girls from the better part of town had connections with a dope peddler from the big city. She had goof-balls and also doped cigarettes. She usually waited until the others were well inebriated before she let them have the marijuana. Some of them didn't know what they were smoking and they didn't care—they just liked the feeling."

Lile was a sadistic creature. Her folks had divorced several years before and she was now living with her mother and rich step-father. Her mother and step-father both drank and gave wild parties which was why they didn't want her around the house at night. It was her reputation as a night streetwalker that got her the dealership for dope.

"When it came my time to smoke one of the marijuanas, I paid for it and lit it. It was different to anything I had experienced before. When I began to feel woozy I got scared and threw the rest of it out the window. They asked me if I didn't like the "weed" and I told them my stomach had been upset that day. And anyway since I hadn't smoked before they didn't pay the incident much mind."

This experience caused Roger to sit up and take stock of himself. He really *was* mixed up in something worse than he had anticipated.

"The preacher told me they didn't stop at dancing, but I thought he was wrong. I didn't think he could know what he was talking about. I knew that he hadn't done those things, so I wondered how he knew. Later I found out that a person doesn't need to participate in such things to know they exist. I was just too dumb and stubborn about the whole matter. But I never would have believed that the club members were dopers if I hadn't seen it with my own eyes. At school they really put on a front. They were considerate and polite and many of the teachers were fooled about them. But away from school and especially on these night rides or club meetings as they called them, they were unpredictable."

The thing that puzzled Roger was that the peddlers should come to a moderate-sized town like Centerville to peddle their stuff. The cities were on the war-path against them, so maybe they were looking for safer territories for awhile. And the thing that was the most astonishing of all was that they were getting away with it. Once a victim got started they wouldn't tell where the cigarettes or capsules came from. Law enforcement against the dope was a difficult task.

"Each time I saw how stupid the others got I wished I'd never heard of the club. I didn't want to smoke or drink or do any of the things the bunch was doing. But I felt that I was too far in now to get out."

In time word finally reached the Horton's about the activities of the No-name Club. The information horrified Grandma Horton and made Grandpa Horton very angry. They had never had such a problem as this with their children so they didn't know what should be their first move. Brother Ainsworth and the elders of the church were called together. Grandpa Horton felt that this problem concerned more than just their home. It involved the church, the school and the community as well.

"We're counting on you, Brother Ainsworth," said Grandpa Horton at the elder's meeting. "You've talked with the boy before, so you're the likely one to talk to him now. And another thing, gentlemen, I've been thinking lately. Somewhere down the line we've let this boy down. I'm his grandfather, but I haven't known what to do with him. I'm afraid I've made a big blunder in Roger's case. As mother and me look back on it, it seems that we began to lose the boy when he started going to those denominational young peoples' parties. Mother and me never played with the boy so I guess he went over there to have fun. Then came the high school dances. You're aware of the fight we had over that subject. It looks like we lost him through his recreation. Most all the other young people were enjoying themselves in some kind of activities, so I guess he had a right to expect some fun too. But we didn't provide anything worthwhile for him. That's why he got away from us. When that boy comes home now he's not the same youngster we used to have. He's growing up fast and we may have lost him for good. But we're hoping your talk with him will put some sense in his head, preacher. Now you go ahead and we're all behind you."

"Brother Ainsworth didn't want to talk with me further. He thought I was beyond help, and I guess I was at the time. I was determined to have some of the pleasures out of life. The trouble was I didn't know what the real pleasures were."

The preacher called Roger and requested another meeting between them. Roger was reluctant to accept the invitation, but he didn't know any way out.

"Brother Ainsworth got to the park before I did. No one else was around when I arrived so I selected a bench out of view. I didn't want anyone to see us there, and especially the gang."

"We'll skip the usual formalities and get right down to the matter at hand. We've been getting reports of the drinking and other activities your club has been participating in lately. I don't need to ask you if the reports are true. I know they are. Centerville is too small a place for that kind of thing to go unnoticed. Your grandparents are very disturbed about your associations and so are the elders of the church. They sent me here to discuss this matter with you. Now what about it, can't you act more like a man and get away from such as that?"

"Look, I got problems and I'll work them out myself. You don't understand my situation. Nobody does. And there's no way you, or the elders, or my grandparents can help me. I just want to be left alone."

"But can you work these problems out by yourself? Most young people have a mother or a daddy to go to when they need help. But you don't have anyone outside of the Horton's, and your grandfather tells me you two don't understand one another. Now I'd like to be a big brother to you, if you'll let me. Working together, we can pull you out of this mess. But I can't do a thing without your cooperation."

"I was getting more confused all the time. The preacher had made me a real good bargain. I could get help to get away from the gang if I wanted it. If I would tell him everything and get it off my chest maybe he could work something out. That would be a grand thing. But I got shaky in the knees when I thought about having to face the club members five days a week at school. They would really make life miserable for me. I didn't believe I could stand that."

In desperation the preacher decided to put some pressure on Roger. He hadn't succeeded in getting anything out of his young friend any other way, so he tried direct charges.

"Roger, are you getting drunk like the other members of your gang? The town's people say you are."

"This question rocked me on my heels. I didn't know the whole town knew what we were doing. The gang said nobody knew. I told the preacher I sipped a little, but that was all."

"And how do you know you won't go further next time and get drunk?" the preacher pressed him.

"Because I don't like the stuff, that's why! I don't drink any more than I have to. I get along with the gang, that's all."

"And how do you know you won't turn out like your father? Maybe he started drinking with a crowd like you're doing. What guarantee do you have that you won't follow in his steps? You could you know."

"I didn't even try to answer him. He was right and I couldn't think of any more to say. But I was sure that I wasn't going to end up like daddy. I was determined not to. Then we finished our talk and shook hands like friends. I wanted to get out of the club like the preacher suggested, but I just couldn't now. I knew too much and there was no telling what they might try to do to me if I tried."

CHAPTER 6

MARGIE AT THE BALL

"BROTHER AINSWORTH wasn't surprised when I returned to the club and the school socials. I guess he was accustomed to seeing young people do crazy things because of the hold a high school group could get on them. I was certainly no exception. I was a slave to all of their petty whims and fancies. And a high school clique can be very unpredictable. By now the preacher knew that I would try to weather this storm out. I didn't think I could get out of the gang if I wanted to, so I chose to take my chances with them."

The preacher was well aware that there was nothing he could say or do to change Roger's current trend of conduct. He did pray daily that he wouldn't get hurt too badly and that in time he would break the captive chains his social friends had put on him. But how long his young friend would remain under the hypnotic spell was a guessing matter.

"For the next few months I was about as unpredictable as the winds of a cyclone. I guess I was quite a mystery to the town. I'm still amazed at how long-suffering the church was with me during this time. Though I didn't take as active a part in my class work and all with the church, still my attendance didn't suffer. The Horton's saw to that. They worked on the theory that if I got the chance to know right from wrong that the day would come when I would return to the right. At least they hoped and prayed that I would."

Though Roger had never made up his mind to seek new companionship, he thought about it. He was suffering an agonizing conflict with the church folks, including the Hortons on one side, and the high school students on the other. Roger's heart was the battleground. He prayed and thought and changed his mind numerous times. He wanted to be good, but he couldn't make up his mind to pay the price. But one night he and Andy Hilton had words and things got unpleasant for each of them. This was his opportunity to get out—at least he had a good excuse. And as he was getting ready to tell the club off and leave, he changed his mind. He remembered Marjorie Scofield and decided to stay in after all.

Marjorie was a very attractive, auburn-haired girl with the most beautiful hazel-blue eyes in the world. She was of medium height and was by far the neatest dresser in school. She and her folks had recently moved to Centerville from New York because her father had been transferred there by a large farm-equipment manufacturing firm. It didn't take Margie long to fit into the social life of the school since any new girl was a treat for the home-town boys.

Roger had seen Margie the first day she visited Centerville High, and he fell for her then, but was too timid to introduce himself.

"Little did I ever dream that she would give me a second glance. I was shy in public and must have made my feelings of inferiority quite evident. But she was lovely and graceful and the image of everything I thought I ever wanted in a girl friend. All the rest of the boys had their eyes on her too, so I expected to be satisfied just admiring her from a distance."

Two weeks later Roger met Margie at the dance, Richard Hutfield was her escort that night and Roger had brought Shirley Hawkins.

"I was just plain rude to Shirley after that. But I couldn't help it. I couldn't keep my eyes off Margie. Then we got better acquainted after the dance when we all drove out to the drive-in. Richard might as well have been dating Shirley that night. Margie and I didn't make any bones about wanting to be together so we just ignored our dates. However, I didn't get to see her much that night. They took her home early because they didn't know whether she would fit into our activities or not."

The girls at school were amazed that the new town beauty should pay any attention at all to Roger, much less accept his invitation to the next Friday night dance. When the girls pressed her for an explanation she told them her reasons quite frankly.

"That boy's going somewhere, girls, and that's the kind of fellow I want. And what about those broad shoulders and that brown wavy hair. And don't you think he's got beautiful eyes? They're a little sad, but I like them anyway. He's also got strong arms and I like men with strength. And who knows, one of these days he's liable to be a real he-man. I like him too, and I guess that's enough reason to date him. But there's another thing I like about Roger. He's not a wolf. All the boys at home are wolves, or at least all I know there. I like a quiet, unassuming boy with some hidden ability. That's my Roger."

"But Margie," one of the girls exclaimed, "Roger's been a dud around town for years. Why he hasn't got a reputation or talent or money or a car or. . . ."

"Hold it right there, sis!" Margie spit back. "Roger's alright for me, besides its none of your business who I date or why. Now you gals go on and peddle your petunias."

Roger smiled when he thought about how he felt during his early dates with Margie. "There I was the nobody-boy, yet I was dating the most sought-after girl in Centerville. Those boys at school sure gave me some hard looks but she was worth them. It didn't take us but about six weeks to convince the rest of the neighborhood that neither of us were available after that. And as for my world, it revolved completely around Margie. There were good reasons too. I can see them now, but I sure didn't understand all of them then. For one thing she stroked my ego. She made me feel really wanted. She used to tell me all the good qualities she saw in me and she made me believe I had them too. This was the first person, outside of Brother Ainsworth, that ever made me feel that I might really have a bright future ahead of me. She gave me self-confidence and made me do things with pride. Really, she was a panacea for nearly all my troubles. By being a congenial companion she helped me forget my loneliness. As a matter of fact she made me forget *all* my past woes. We were too busy talking about each other and the future. We liked the same foods, same entertainment, and same movie stars. I had never known a person who understood me as Margie did."

The abrupt change in Roger showed itself in several ways.

For one, he no longer craved the crowds and the excitement of gay parties. Now he was content to be alone with Margie.

"We got off to ourselves every chance we got and used the time to make plans. It was lots of fun talking about what we were going to do after school was out. And so far as I was concerned the parties and dances in Centerville could all fold up. I had what I wanted and I didn't care about anything else."

Back at the church house, Brother Ainsworth was wrestling with the problem of what to do about his wandering adolescent friends.

"You see, Brother Hendley, you're an elder of this church and any move among the parents of the congregation should be instigated by you and the other elders. This isn't a church project, but a home effort. What these folks need is leadership and there should be no finer leaders anywhere in such a good work as this as the elders of God's church. Now you'll agree that when you were young you wanted a good time. That's natural for youngsters in their adolescent years. Where we're falling down today is that we're not meeting new competition. There's a lot more in the way of outside-the-home entertainment now than when we were growing up. And a great deal of this outside entertainment isn't wholesome. Some of it might be good within itself, but ungodly people in the world have taken it over so that Christians can't engage in it for fear of harming their influence. Now here's my position. Young people don't want questionable recreation any more than we want them to have it. But they do want something! And they have a right to have something! If we or some other good people don't provide them with decent fun, what's left but the questionable and the downright sinful recreation?"

"But Brother Ainsworth, I don't see that our young people are such a problem. We don't have but one or two here that are out of line. Why should that disturb us so?"

"Why should that disturb us? What if it were your son? Would that disturb you?"

"Well, if you put it that way, I guess it would."

"And even if we had only one case, but lost that young person, wouldn't that be enough to cause us some concern? I'm going to be frank with you Brother Hendley. We're losing our young people from the home and the church too through their recreation. They have more leisure time today than you and I ever dreamed of having. Now what are they to do with it? They don't know all the answers. They need help. They want help. But up until now we've been too busy with adult matters to pay much attention to our kids. That's why we're losing them. They look to us for help and we're letting them down. That's why I can't be too critical of Roger Scott. That kid's had a hard time and just between you and me, his grandfather and grandmother have done their very best, but that just wasn't good enough. That kid's gone back into the world and whether or not we'll ever get him back is questionable. Now what we need to do is give these kids more good, solid, genuine home life. The parents of the congregation need to quit being so selfish. They need to be buddies to their children. I'm not even married yet, but I can see that. And the church can help a lot too."

"How can the church help young man? We're ready to do all we can."

"The church can help by giving these boys and girls a chance to participate actively in the work of the church. We need to give our boys a chance to learn to lead public prayer and lead singing. The girls can help in the benevolent phase of the work. They can visit the sick and prepare food for needy families. Together, the young people can have painting parties and brighten up some of our drab-looking classrooms. Kids need things gay and cheerful. They want to be a part of the church, but we just haven't let them feel that they belong. That's all I think they want—just to feel that they belong."

"Then we'll call the meeting you're asking for. We'll get these parents together and see if we can't work something out. Maybe we can't get Roger back, but we'll try to keep any others from following his lead."

"Thank you, Brother Hendley. And I assure you you'll never regret it."

The elders of the Lord's church at Centerville called a special meeting of all mothers and fathers of adolescents. The session took place in the home of Brother Hendley.

"I don't know what all Brother Ainsworth said to those parents, but the elders agreed wholeheartedly and the parents came home very enthusiastic. Grandpa and Grandma seemed quite cheerful about it. I found out later that the parents agreed to start giving more attention to the needs of their children. And after that meeting, things really began to happen. Backyards were equipped with barbecue pits and tables and chairs. Lawns were lighted for outdoor recreation at night and the members began to open their homes up to the young people more. Then there was the Green family who had a large empty room in their home. They let the church kids come over and paint it to suit themselves and let that be their game room. The room was cleaned and painted red, white and blue, according to their vivid imagination. One of the men in the congregation was a carpenter so he made two ping-pong tables for the game room and some smaller tables for quieter games. Soon there were enough donated tables and chairs to comfortably furnish the room."

Sister Greene's spare room made quite a hit with the young people. And she was quite popular with them too, being a jovial person who loved to make cookies for young people and serve iced drinks on hot days. But whenever she had to be in town she merely hung out her sign, 'Come back later, please' and the young people respected it. She never allowed the young folks in her home when she wasn't present.

"The new recreational plan included outdoor activities as well as indoor. When Brother Ainsworth explained the idea to our class I liked it from the start. When he mentioned fishing trips, picnics, and hikes I got interested. I had wanted to do all those things all the time, but Grandpa never felt like it any more. In addition to these get-togethers the preacher handed every member of the class a list of activities and we were allowed to choose what we would do that week. The list included:

> barbecues
> progressive dinners
> hamburger feeds
> hay rides
> treasure hunts

tacky parties
horseback riding
scavenger hunts
wild-life expeditions
steak frys
sight-seeing tours
bicycle hikes
roller skating
tramp parties
ice cream suppers
watermelon feeds
banquets

But this was only the beginning. In addition to all these activities the group of young people began driving to nearby towns for Sunday afternoon church singings, and gospel meetings. Occasionally they met with groups from other churches of Christ and had ball games on Saturday afternoon after a picnic. Too, they started visiting the sick members of the church and singing a few songs to them. In the summer time some of them went off to the Vacation Bible School camps and a few of them went to the singing normals."

It wasn't long until the young people in the church at Centerville didn't miss the pleasures of the world at all. They were too busy enjoying Christian association with other young people of the church.

"Once all these activities got started Brother Ainsworth came to me and urged me to change my mind about the gang and to start going around with the church group. I told him I would think about it and did, but I decided not to quit the club at school. I thought I had really grown up since I met Margie. Now I was going steady and felt much too sophisticated to act like a kid again. And too, in her field, Margie was tops. She was the life of the party; she had been around. She knew how to control a group and when she got through with them she had them wrapped around her little finger. I just didn't think she would fit in with our group at the church at all."

Margie's great popularity caused most the high school clubs to send her an invitation for membership, but she stayed with the No-name Club. Roger didn't understand why at first, but later he found out.

"I was very embarrassed and ashamed the first time the gang offered Margie a drink. Since she was my idol I didn't think she would do anything like that. But she did. She took the bottle and showed even the boys a thing or two about drinking. That sure disappointed me, but there wasn't much I could do about it. She drank and smoked both without my knowing it at first. There's no question about it, she really had me fooled with that false front."

The Horton's had heard rumors down town to the effect that Roger and Margie planned to get married secretly sometime soon, so they were distressed about it. Adverse gossip had been circulating through the usual channels about Margie for some time. Her parents had no reputation at all among the church people. They were steady drinkers and were seen about town drunk once in a great while. That didn't sound good to the Horton's at all. The reports were that the Scofields had already granted their permission for Margie to marry Roger any time she wanted to, so the Horton's were afraid they might before he was through school. They knew Roger would have a hard enough time getting a good job with a high school education. Above all, they wanted to see him get his high school diploma.

"Grandpa called Brother Ainsworth and tried to get him to see me again, but the preacher didn't want to."

"I know, preacher, but we got to try to do something. That boy hasn't breathed a word about getting married to grandmother or me. He's the tightest lipped kid I ever saw. He doesn't tell us anything. We thought maybe he'd talk with you again. Just get him to promise not to quit school. We'll settle for that. If he will, you tell him I'll give him a handsome graduation gift, say $100.00 cash."

"Yes sir, I'll tell him, but I warn you, Roger isn't listening to anybody but Margie these days."

"Say, wait a minute. You say Roger won't listen to anyone but Margie? Then why not talk to Margie. Surely she can see the wisdom in waiting awhile. No girl wants to marry a boy who can't support her. Approach her from that angle. Maybe it'll work."

Roger went over to a neighboring town the following Sunday afternoon with a gang of boys. So Brother Ainsworth took this opportunity to talk with Margie alone. He called her first and then went to her house. She invited him in and as he entered he sensed the strong smell of beer and tobacco smoke. He wondered to himself if this was truly the kind of home Roger wanted. The ensuing conversation lasted about twenty minutes. The preacher was frank but kind as he presented his views.

"Margie, surely you and Roger realize the folly of your marrying before you get out of school. Today a high school diploma is worth no more than a grammar school certificate was twenty years ago. Why even a B.A. degree from college is considered little better than a high school diploma fifteen years ago or so. Competition is getting stronger all the time, and if Roger doesn't have a minimum of a high school diploma he will have a hard time finding the kind of job that pays anything. Now you don't want to marry a boy who can't provide an average home for you, do you?"

"Look here. Roger and I are going to get married. We love each other. And that's settled. But if you say his folks will help him get a start financially if we wait till summer, then maybe we'll consider the matter. Maybe we'll wait till then to have the wedding."

"I think you're being smart, Margie. Any girl in her right mind would rather sacrifice a little time with her boy friend for a stable life with him later."

"You don't need to concern yourself about Roger and me, nor about his future. He'll make out fine. I'm seeing to that."

"What do you mean? How can you help him?"

"My father has connections in New York. He knows a lot of people there, see. As a matter of fact Roger already has a chance at a good job there. Dad has already asked for it for Roger."

The Horton's were relieved when they heard the good news about the wedding date, but they were very disappointed to learn that Roger planned to leave Centerville after graduation. They had hoped that he would stay close so they could keep watch over him.

"The Spring months were passing very rapidly for us now and Margie and I both began to realize that our high school life would soon be a thing of the past. This settled both of us down a lot. Our grades got better because we took more time to study and we always studied together. After this we didn't give anyone any trouble. Everyone seemed to appreciate it and the Principal even took notice of it and complimented Margie and me one day as we were strolling across the school grounds."

Graduation night finally came. Margie was seated next to Roger since her name was Scofield and his was Scott. They were very proud of themselves that night. They were sitting on top of the world when their "sheep-skins" were presented to them.

"When the graduation exercises were over we felt that we had a new lease on life. Somehow we felt that we had a new-born freedom which elevated us above the advice and suggestions of others. We felt educated now. We had our diplomas! What else was there to learn?"

Roger stayed at the Horton's place a few days after graduation, but he was anxious to get on his way so he was packing all the time.

"I began to really feel funny now. It wouldn't be long until I would leave home and that thought made me kinda uneasy. Another thing I wanted to do before I left was to make up to the folks for the way I had treated them. I tried to be considerate and understanding and catered to their wishes all I could. They realized what I was trying to do and they did everything possible to make my last few days pleasant ones. When I wasn't at home with the folks I was out with Margie making plans for our wedding. But after a few days of this I began to get restless. A few days before, I was being honored as a June high school graduate, but now I felt like an unemployed bum."

Grandpa Horton took Roger aside the night before he was to leave for New York. He tried to give him all the fatherly advice he would need in a strange city. "Roger, you're a mighty young man to be going all the way to New York by yourself to find work. There's work around here and I can help you get a job."

"I know, Grandpa, but Margie's father got me this job and I guess I'd better take it. Anyway, I want to get away from Centerville. Maybe, someday we'll come back here to live."

"But Roger, you don't know a thing about the big city. There's all kind of trouble you can get into. Up there they play for keeps. Once you get in trouble up there they'd as soon kill you as look at you. You know that. Grandma and me just don't want you to get into the wrong company up there and get yourself hurt."

Roger was adamant. He didn't intend to change any of his plans at this late date and he convinced Grandpa Horton that this was so.

"Alright son, if that's the way its gotta be, then your grandmother and me want to help you. Here's a hundred dollars to help you get started on. And if things get too tough up there you know you can come home to us any time."

"I accepted the hundred dollars reluctantly. 'Thanks a lot, grandpa, but do you think I deserve this money? I've been a pretty hard fellow to get along with you know'."

"Yes son, I know, but mama and me feel like we're partly to blame. You can forget all about the trouble you've been to us. You've been a blessing to us too, you know. It was good to have a youngster around the house. It kept us from being so lonely without our kids. But just one other thing. Take your Bible with you and read it every day. And too, find the church up there as soon as you arrive and don't neglect the services. You'll need them up there by yourself. And the Christian people will be your friends and can help you out a lot. We think you've got a fairly good background now and we hope you don't let it go to waste. Just stay close to the Lord and his Book and His people and you'll get through life successfully. Then one of these days we're going to be real proud of you and we can say we helped a little to make a fine man out of you."

"My departure the next day wasn't as pleasant as I had thought it would be. For months I had been waiting eagerly for this time, but now that it was here I dreaded it. When I got down to the station I remembered the day I first stepped onto that platform. I was scared and I cried because I hadn't wanted to come. Now I was uneasy again, but this time I didn't want to leave. I was sorry I was going away."

The Hortons and Margie went to the station with Roger. When the train came into sight he bade his grandparents goodbye and they went back to the car.

"Margie, I'll do the very best I can for you in New York. I'll save my money and we'll get married soon—real soon. I love you very much. And I want you to be with me more than anything else in the world."

"And I love you too, Roger. I'll be waiting for your call. Work hard, honey. There's a lot at stake, but I know you can do it. I've always believed in you and I know you'll never let me down. Goodbye, darling. I'll be anxiously awaiting your letters."

"Then I reluctantly boarded the train. Margie looked around at me once and waved and ran home crying. I was crying too."

CHAPTER 7

MR. AND MRS. ROGER SCOTT

"I was sick when the train pulled out of the Centerville station that morning. Partings were always hard on me. They brought back bad memories. But this trip was especially difficult because I was leaving the most precious girl in the world. I loved her and she loved me and we had vowed to never be apart. Yet, we were now. Then I'll never forget the miseries of that day and the day after that as the train sped on toward New York. Each mile took me farther away from Margie and at times I felt that this would be more than I could stand."

The years that Roger had spent at the Horton's place had left him some tender memories. The bitter ones were all but forgotten now. But Roger's heart struck him a savage blow when he thought how foolishly he had acted in defying his grandparents and Brother Ainsworth. Now that the smoke was cleared away from the battlefield he could see his folly more clearly. Things that meant so much to him those junior and senior years in high school were child's play to him now. Everything was serious these days. But now he was out on his own and was about to get his first job and start making a living for his bride-to-be.

"I guess my face must have flushed a dozen times a day as I sat on that train and reflected on my stupidity at Centerville. Those people must have thought I was a little weak in the brain sure enough. Maybe they were right. But if they weren't, they would have been right in concluding that I was weak in conscience and conviction. My record wasn't an enviable one."

The train was getting farther away from Centerville all the time as it sped through Kentucky, West Virginia and then Pennsylvania.

"I was seeing a lot of new and different scenery along the way and thousands of new faces every day. Yet, I was extremely lonely. At this time I would have given up my hundred dollars just to see somebody from Centerville—anybody."

As the train drew closer to New York City Roger began bracing himself for the ordeal ahead. He had never been to the big city and he wasn't sure how well he would make out without someone to help him.

"When we got into seeing-distance of the skycrapers I became a little amused to think that I wouldn't be here if I had taken the preacher's advice. He advised me to stay in Centerville as strongly as Grandpa did. He also insisted that I was passing up the opportunity of a life-time by not going to a Christian College. He even had Grandpa agree to help me through, but I wouldn't hear to it. No sir, I'd been twelve years getting out and now I was going to stay out. Besides, I wanted to get married more than anything else. Four more years was too long to wait. I don't think Margie would have waited on me anyway. All we wanted was some quick money and to get married."

Finally after several delays in the outskirts of the city, Roger's train wormed its way into the great spiderweb of rail yards outside of Grand Central Station.

"I could tell we were nearly there because we moved along the rails so slowly. When the train jolted to a halt I was already on the platform anxious to get off. Then when they opened the doors it was quite a sight to behold. Strangers by the hundreds and thousands came pouring through the station doors and rushed up to the train. I must have been quite a sight because the best I can remember I just stood there with my mouth open glaring at this ocean of weaving humanity. I had never seen so many people in all my life and I couldn't figure out where they could have come from."

Roger stepped out of the coach and into the stream of human traffic. He flowed along with them until they scattered onto the streets of New York. Once outside the station he stopped again and gazed at his surroundings in amazement.

"I had never seen anything like this before. I must have made a funny sight there—just a teen-age kid bewildered and

102

gawking at the bright lights. Finally, when I got my breath back I started down the sidewalk, then I stepped back out of the way. Hundreds of people were rushing past and pushing each other around. None of them seemed the worse nor did any of them take offense. Then just as I was getting ready to start out again a swarm of red-caps spotted me. We had a little tussle but I won out and convinced them that I didn't need help. But no sooner had I gotten my luggage away from the red-caps when the taxi drivers began grabbing for it. However, I evaded them without too much trouble and went on across the street to get my breath and bearings."

What Roger saw then bewildered him. There were lights everywhere, all shapes and colors as the giant neon signs flashed out their informative messages.

"I guess I got a little dizzy as I stood there trying to figure out the whole pattern of this great metropolis. I wasn't accustomed to the hundreds of cars and taxi cabs whizzing by the curbs. This surely was a contrast to Centerville where most people went their way without much fuss or bother. Then I remembered I didn't know a soul in New York and didn't know where to go for food or lodging. Margie had told me about some places but I didn't have the slightest idea how to find any of them. But when I remembered how hungry I was I set out to find me a cafe."

After a warm and nourishing supper Roger felt considerably better. By now he had collected his wits and located a small room down the street from the train station where he could stay until he located his work the following Monday.

"Monday was slow about coming around. I got to New York on Saturday night and found an eating place and a room, but I didn't have much luck the next day finding a congregation of the church of Christ. I wandered about the streets till noon and same in the afternoon. Then I asked around, but never did find the church building. The rest of the afternoon and night was spent riding the subways. That too was a new and fascinating experience for me."

Roger went to work early Monday morning. He hadn't remembered what time he was scheduled to report but he took no chances in being late. He was eager to make a good first impression so he left his room at 6:30 that morning.

"I took a taxi just to be sure I got to the right address and arrived there about 7:30. My destination must not have been more than ten or fifteen blocks away, but it took us nearly an hour to get there. Seems like we went a 'round-about route. When I got in the cab I just gave him the address Margie's father had given me and set back to enjoy the ride. When the cab got to the address I had given, I found that we were in front of Saponie's Dress Shop. I wondered for a moment whether this was right or not, but finally paid the cabbie and sent him on his way."

Roger checked the address on the slip of paper to varify that this shop was the place. However, the doors were closed and judging by the mail which lay just inside the mail slot in the door there hadn't been anyone there in several days.

"When I saw all that mail stacked up and the untidiness of the shop I began to wonder if I had a job. It looked like the place was closed. But I decided to wait around—mainly because I didn't have anything else to do. By noon I was really worried. Still no one came to the shop. By now I was almost sure the Saponies had gone out of business, but upon inquiring down the street the merchants assured me they would be back. They told me I might have a long wait however."

About mid-afternoon a group of people arrived at the shop much to Roger's relief. They came down the sidewalk talking loudly and went into the shop without as much as glancing at the worried-looking kid out in front.

"I was uneasy when I stepped inside the door and asked for Mr. Saponie. When I found him I handed him the letter Mr. Scofield had written for me as an introduction."

"Do you mean to tell me, young man, that you have come all the way from Centerville to New York to get this job? Why, son, I just mentioned to Mr. Scofield that I had an opening. I didn't ask for anyone. There are plenty of unemployed people here in the city who can take this job. As a matter of fact I hired a man three weeks ago."

"But Margie told me that her daddy wrote you to hold the job open for me! She said it was an open and shut matter, that you and her daddy were old friends and that you would save the job as a favor to him."

"That may all be true, son, but I didn't get his letter, if he wrote one. And if I did it would be one of the few he ever wrote me. He just doesn't write much. But I'll tell you what. I'll put you on for a few days just to help you over the hump until you can find a job. How's that?"

"Oh, thank you sir. That'll help. But I can't figure why you haven't heard from Mr. Scofield. Margie told me several times that he was going to write you. Why, I never would have come all the way up here if I hadn't thought I had a job waiting for me. Guess I'll learn not to rely on everybody else to tend to my business, won't I?"

"That's just one of those things, boy. And you're right! Never trust anyone else to do what you can do for yourself. I found that out the hard way too—many years ago."

So Roger went to work for the Saponie Dress Shop. He ran errands, swept out the shop and kept the cloth trimmings out of the seamstresses way. These menial tasks were extremely unsavory and were quite a blow to his ego.

"Here I was sweeping and running my legs off carrying dress samples around. I thought I had a job in a machine shop or in construction or something. Why I ever took the job for granted will always be a puzzle to me. I guess I just put too much confidence in Margie's word and she trusted her father too far. But my ego took the severest blow at the end of the week when I got paid. Fifteen dollars was all I got. That barely took care of my meals and my room and didn't leave me a thing for our savings."

The Saponies were an erratic and undesirable people to work for. They owned the dress shop and ran it almost entirely on family help. They worked when they felt like it and took off when they wanted to.

"They took off several days at a time when Brooklyn was playing in town. And Mr. Saponie seldom missed a major-league game. He watched the Giants and Yankees about equal, but deserted both of them when the Dodgers were playing. I got to see a few of the games, but never when the 'big ones' came along. I got to use the pass only when the weaker visiting teams were in town."

The Saponies were all fat because of overindulgence. They worked hard while at the shop and feasted as hard at home after hours. Most of them had quick tempers and they cursed and swore at one another off and on most of the time. Sometimes their orders for dresses came in abundance and sometimes they would come slowly. Whenever they got their bank account looking respectable, however, they went on a spree for several days.

"It was on one of those spree-days that I got so disgusted with them. I was invited to their home out of courtesy in the first place. I felt obliged to go due to their kindness to me, but I was soon sorry I accepted the invitation. They just don't live like civilized people should. They lived in a big house with fine furniture and antiques and all, but their manners were everything but cultured after they got drunk. They insisted that I drink with them and I did a little to be polite, but I didn't like it. But they did! They laughed big when I choked on the whiskey and got red in the face. This especially delighted Mr. Saponie. He was a big kidder anyway and he laughed until tears rolled down his cheeks. I was greatly humiliated but there was little I could do at the time but grin and bear it."

Roger was unhappy with his job and employers. He had now been in New York several weeks and had been humiliated and embarrassed numerous times. He didn't like being a delivery boy for one thing. He thought a high school graduate should have more dignified opportunities for service. Too, he disliked his drinking companions. Occasionally they continued their drinking at the shop and made working conditions unpleasant.

"I had been looking for a job as opportunities presented themselves but hadn't located a thing after several weeks. But one day as I was leaning against a lamp-post in front of the shop a man approached me with a proposition to work for him. He

106

owned the laundry down the street and when his drivers went on a strike he fired half of them. He said he got rid of all the troublemakers. Naturally I was interested so I gave the Saponies a few hours notice and quit. The working conditions at the laundry were much more to my liking. At least I had something definite to do all the time. That standing around in the shop waiting for something to do was getting on my nerves."

There was nothing exciting about Roger's new job, but he liked it. He had his own truck and had been given a zone. He picked up dirty clothes and delivered them back the next day. Some of the other drivers were hateful at times and picked at him, but this didn't bother Roger much since he was away from the laundry on deliveries most of the time.

"With steady work and regular pay I got to feeling better about our wedding plans. Now I was saving a little each week out of my check and I knew we would soon have enough to get married. I wasn't sure how much money it took to get married, but I knew Margie wanted a nice wedding."

Margie had written Roger nearly every day since he left Centerville. Her letters were a source of strength to him through his trying times with the Saponies. And Roger made his nightly pilgrimages to his shrine—his wabbly writing table where he wrote long replies to Margie's letters. His reports back were a little more glowing than the facts justified. And because of the general impression he left in his letters, everyone at home was resting easier now that he was settled and happy.

"When my account at the bank got to $300 Margie began hinting about our marriage date. They were gentle reminders at first, but soon began to be more insistent. She was getting impatient and was showing signs of irritation. Finally she wrote me a desperate letter."

"Dear Roger,

Why do you keep putting off our marriage? Don't you still love me? Or have you found someone there you like better? Tell me truthfully. If there isn't someone else, or something like that, then I see no reason for delaying our plans any longer. I'm sick and tired of laying around the house taking orders from mother and dad. I want to get out on my own like you are. We'll both like it better that way. But I mean business. If you don't start doing something about our wedding pretty soon I'm going to start looking around for a boy who really wants a wife. I hope you can do something soon—for your sake.

With all my love,
Margie"

"The threat in Margie's letter sent cold chills racing up and down my spine. The mere thought of losing her gave me a peculiar weak feeling in the pit of my stomach. So I decided to do something quick. Above all I wanted Margie happy. I began making arrangements to return to Centerville right away. I got a substitute driver for my route and got some money out of the bank. Then I bought my ticket at the railroad station."

Roger's train left New York at 5 o'clock Friday afternoon. He was relieved. He had put Margie off a little longer than he wanted to because he wanted to be sure he had enough money for their wedding and their honeymoon afterwards.

"I was sitting on top of the world when I got to my seat on the coach and realized fully that I was on my way home. And much to my surprise I was very anxious to see everybody there and all the familiar sites. I guess I hadn't realized how much I missed the folks in Centerville until I began to anticipate seeing them again. I had been gone from Margie only a few months but they seemed like years. But now I felt like it was all worth it. I wanted a beautiful wedding to do justice to the most beautiful bride in town."

Roger was home only two days before the wedding. He and Margie worked feverishly during that time getting everything ready. Finally, the grand hour came. Brother Ainsworth officiated and the wedding took place in the auditorium at the church house. There was a background of greenery which was flanked by stands of beautiful pink gladiolas. It wasn't a long ceremony, nor too elaborate, but it was highly impressive to Roger.

"Dearly beloved, we are gathered here in the sight of God and in the presence of this company to unite in marriage these two young people."

"It was God, the Father, who in the long ago said that it is not good for man to live alone. Therefore, He created woman to be a helpmeet to man. She was created from the flesh in man's side and was placed beside man as his companion and not as his slave. She was then flesh of his flesh and bone of his bone. Man and woman were no longer twain but one flesh. And God commanded that whatsoever he had joined together no man should put asunder."

"Husbands have been commanded by the Christ to love their wives even as Christ also loved the church and gave himself for it. Even so ought husbands to love their wives as their own selves. He that loveth his wife loveth himself."

"A worthy woman is a crown to her husband. Her price is far above rubies. The heart of the husband trusteth in her and she will do him good all the days of his life."

"The relationships of marriage fulfill the needs, deep in the heart of man. Each person supplies the wants and needs of the other. Each is a strength to the other's weakness, thus making one strong man. And in this union man finds his greatest happiness, as well as the peace of mind and comfort of heart which he craves."

"Marriage is not a moral contract to be broken at the will of either of you or both of you. It is a sacred provision of God and was His first ordinance to man."

"When God united the first man and the first woman in holy wedlock He also created the first home. Now another home is to be founded. There will be joys to share and sorrows to bear."

"Who gives this woman away?"

Mr. Scofield said "I do" and retired to his seat next to his wife.

The preacher then directed Roger and Margie to join their right hands.

"Roger, do you take Margie to be your lawful wedded wife

109

and promise to be true to her in sickness and in health, in prosperity and adversity according to the ordinances of God?"

"I replied 'I do' and gave Margie's hand a gentle squeeze."

"And Margie, do you take Roger as your lawful wedded husband and promise to be true to him in sickness and in health, in prosperity and adversity according to the ordinances of God?"

"Margie looked at me and said 'I do'. I think that was the sweetest expression I have ever seen on anyone's face. For a moment I wondered if I was marrying a mortal or an angel."

"Then after the exchanging of rings and the prayer the preacher concluded the ceremony."

"In the hearing of this company you have pledged your troth each to the other. God in Heaven is also a witness to your vows. You have been joined in hand and you are now joined in heart. And now by the laws of this state I pronounce you husband and wife and may the Lord abundantly bless and keep you all the days of your life."

"Everyone was gay at the simple reception given us at the Horton's home. Margie and I were beaming, but I was by far the happiest person there. At long last I had someone to love me and also someone I could love with a limitless devotion. I thought now that my dreary days were over and that lonesomeness would be a thing of the past."

Margie was happy too. Her marriage to Roger meant freedom. She was glad to get away from home and the parental supervision she despised. Now she expected to stay out as late as she wanted to at night and to sleep as long in the mornings as she pleased. In short, she was planning a gay life back in the big city. She entered into the marriage contract with the idea of unrestrained and glamorous times ahead. She had paid little attention to the new obligations and responsibilities she would face as a wife and mother.

"As soon as the reception was over Margie and I visited with Grandpa and Grandma Horton and Brother Ainsworth awhile and then it was train time. We caught the 3:47 from the south and were on our way. Both of us were very happy over the prospects of our new life together. And throughout the trip we acted like the adolescents that we were. I guess it was pretty easy to see that we were newlyweds. Most of the others on the pullman smiled at us, but we didn't pay anyone much attention. We were too busy planning our good times in New York and laying the foundation for the perfect marriage and a happy home."

CHAPTER 8

BUILDING A NEST TOGETHER

"MARGIE AND I arrived at our little New York apartment tired and sleepy after the long journey. For the most part, our trip was enjoyable, but the riding got monotonous toward the last. I guess our apartment wasn't as nice and tidy as I had thought it was. When Margie saw it disappointment showed all over her face. Probably my reports home were a little too much exaggerated. However, she took the shock bravely and didn't say anything."

Margie settled down to be a good housewife for Roger. In a few days she had bought numerous little things for their rooms and had the apartment looking much brighter. And in between their fixing and painting in the apartment they were going out to view the city and to enjoy themselves. It was the Friday night before Roger was due back at work that Margie begged him to extend their honeymoon.

"Please Roger, don't go back to work so soon. We've just gotten the place fixed up so let's take next week off too and have a good time. You promised me you know. And I'm just dying to go down on Broadway. We can make a swanky night spot or two and maybe we can attend one of the theaters."

"I'd like to be off another week, honey, but we're kinda running low on cash. I'm trying to keep at least a hundred dollars in our checking account. And besides, if I don't get back on the job I might not have one before long."

"Alright, alright, go on back to work, but a girl's got a right to a decent honeymoon. Here we've come into this dump and fixed it up to where we can live in it and I want some fun now. Come on, sweetheart, you said you'd show me a good time— just a few more days off and then you can work all you want to."

"Well, I took the next week off. But I checked in at the laundry and made sure my substitute was willing to work for me. Then we started into the wildest week I ever spent. Margie was on familiar ground and she knew most of the spots. In the day time we visited interesting places such as the Empire State Building, the R C A radio center and the docks down by the river. And at night we made the night spots and dined and danced until the early hours of the morning. Then we slept till noon the next day. Margie really loved the glitter of the bright lights. She liked the blaring brass instruments in the dance bands along cafe society. She had grown up with this kind of life and it was in her blood. She thrived on thrills and excitement. She told me this was the life she wanted and she was sure I would give it to her—that's why she picked *me*. This was all new to me and I got to wondering about Margie. I wondered if she was like this all the time or if this was just a passing fancy. But judging by all the friends of hers we met, I decided she was familiar with nearly all the hangouts."

Roger enjoyed the drama and suspense of New York life for a few nights, but after he had seen some of it the rest was mere repetition. A new restaurant, a new dance band and a new head waiter, but the same old routine. Just a smoke-filled dining room and a dance floor full of people.

"The following Monday I went back to work. When I came in after nine hours of work I was too tired to go out so I ate supper and went to bed. Margie waited patiently for me to get accustomed to my old routine then began to plan some more nights out. She wanted to plan our budget so that we could go out at least two nights a week. I tried to reason with her and show her that dinners and floor shows didn't fit into my salary very well. But we finally compromised and went out once each week for awhile."

This limited schedule didn't satisfy Margie however. She had visions of great fun in the big city with her new husband, but she forgot that he didn't make the kind of money her father did. Her hours in the apartment were long ones to her and she expected more of Roger at nights than he could give. She had couples lined up to visit for weeks ahead. And when he was too tired many nights to go anywhere she got irritable and complained of her dull life.

"I tried to be as patient with her as possible. I loved her dearly and wanted more than anything else to see her happy, but there were bounds. I petted her and brought her little things frequently, but those things weren't enough. She was wanting to live above our means and I was trying hard to keep our rent and grocery bills paid. But in time my patience wore thin too. Her constant nagging and complaining began to get on my nerves. I was doing the best I could and I resented her reminders that she might have done better had she married someone else."

" 'I could have had any boy in Centerville and you know it. And some of them were from very wealthy families,' Margie told me."

"Why didn't you marry one of them then, why did you pick on me?"

"Sometimes I wonder now. I really wonder. But now that its done I guess we'll just have to make the best of it."

"I had hoped that maybe in six months or so I would have a better job and could give Margie a better time, but nothing developed. I still had the laundry route and it only paid enough to take care of our necessities. But that didn't stop Margie. She opened several charge accounts at the downtown department stores and got rid of her blues by shopping for new clothes. And the deeper we got in debt the harder it was for us to get along smoothly. I kept trying to slow her down, but she said she didn't have anything else to do. And in time it became evident that our relationship was getting worse rather than better. I was alarmed at how suddenly our perfect marriage started toward the rocks. Then I knew that in time our living together would become unbearable if something wasn't done."

A possible solution came to their attention one afternoon as Margie was scanning the help-wanted column. There was a big ad concerning some good railroad jobs in the middlewest.

"We thought that maybe this was what we were waiting for. The requirements weren't too high. They called for a high school diploma, a willingness to work and the desire to settle with a good company for a long time. Margie helped me write the telegram and we asked for more details. The return telegram a few hours later told us that I could probably find a job if I was over seventeen and out of high school."

The next day Roger quit his job at the laundry. Margie was in a hurry to get into something new so they took the next train out for the little midwest railroad town of Westvalley. The trip took two days and two nights but they thought the new opportunity was worth the ride.

"We liked the looks of Westvalley alright. All the houses were built very much alike and were painted a medium yellow because of the train smoke. Most of the houses were small but they were well kept and the majority of them had nice board fences around the yard and beautiful flower gardens. We went to the employment office the first thing and found out where our house was to be. One of the office clerks directed us down a row of houses on Landsford street and finally pointed to a little four-room cottage. Within a few hours a crew of men moved company furniture in and we were living comfortably in our own little house."

Everything was a buzz the next few days for Roger and Margie. Many of the merchants sent gifts to the house and welcomed the Scotts to open accounts with their stores. And the people were friendly too. Several neighbors dropped by each day to welcome the new couple to the town.

"Margie appreciated the hospitality, but was rather embarrassed by all this kindness. She had grown up in a big city where only a very few close neighbors were friendly. She made the remark one afternoon that she had married to get out of a small town and here she was back in one again. However, there wasn't much she could complain about. Most of the people in town were employees of the railroad so the town was more like one big happy family. Of course, everyone knew nearly everyone else's business, but that was just one of the many characteristics of a small town."

Following the merchants and neighbors came the church people to pay their respects to Roger and Margie. Each of them invited the new couple to their services and informed them

115

of their weekly schedule. Roger waited but no one from the church of Christ came by. He found out later that there was no congregation of the church in Westvalley. The nearest congregation was about 27 miles away. Roger wondered why someone hadn't started one here before, but then dismissed the matter from his mind. He and Margie graciously accepted each gesture of friendship and promised each caller that they would visit their services sometime.

"The First National Bank invited us to open an account with them and the Reliable Loan Company offered to make our first loan for only 3% interest. The Personality Beauty Shoppe sent Margie a gift certificate for one free get-acquainted permanent. Folks in Westvalley made living there so pleasant that no one could help feeling wanted."

At this point Roger stood equal to all men. Here was a chance to begin over. No one knew of his past blunders so they could be forgotten. He was in position now to go as high in his fellowman's estimation as he desired to go. His success or failure from here on would rest squarely on his own shoulders. No one knew about his past and no one cared. Here was his chance to become Roger Scott, respected citizen and promising young business man.

"I liked my work in the traffic control office at the railroad station. It was something new and presented a real challenge to make good. I was determined to do that, and Margie had pledged herself to help me. The two of us were very happy."

"No Roger, that's where you're wrong. I haven't told you yet, but there's going to be three of us—you and me and Billy, or will it be Betty? Anyway I'm so thrilled, Roger. Just think! We're going to have a little boy or girl of our own!"

"Oh Margie, that's wonderful, wonderful news! That's great, in fact! Have you told everybody I'm going to become a father? If not, nevermind, I'll tell them myself. Me, a father! What do you know about that? Roger Scott, a father. Won't that be something! I just can't wait. And I want a boy or a girl, that's what I want!"

"Crazy! What are you talking about? What else could it be but a boy or a girl? What do you expect?"

116

"I mean I don't care whether its a boy or a girl, just so its one of them. No, maybe they'll be twins—a boy *and* a girl. Yeah, that would be something, wouldn't it. Anyway I just can't wait!"

The time passed by rapidly and weeks turned into months. Both Roger and Margie were busy with their jobs, he at the station and she around the house and in the flower and vegetable gardens.

"Finally our big day came. Margie presented me with a fine 6 pound 3 ounce boy. We had already decided to name him Billy Leroy Scott if it was a boy. We were supremely happy now. The next few months went by fast as we petted and pampered our new offspring. We showed him off to all the merchants downtown and to any curious neighbors who happened down our street."

"Just look at that chest, and those muscles in his arms. See, look how he holds his head up. He looks like his father, doesn't he?"

Margie usually nodded when Roger was showing Billy off and let his father do his boasting unrestrained.

"Everything went extremely well for us until Billy was over a year old. It was then that I got the promotion in the office. I got a raise in salary, but the job had one drawback. I had to change to the night shift. That meant I would be away from Margie and Billy at night and do my sleeping in the daytime. Margie and I talked it over and finally agreed that the extra money would be worth the inconveniences."

Time, which had been Margie's friend, now became her enemy. She was alone much of the time with Billy and the change began to show on her nerves. The young couple had made no close friends in the town so she didn't have anyone to chum around with.

"Margie's lack of companionship proved a dangerous thing. For some reason she never took up with anyone in the town much. In a way I always thought she resented the small town. That's why she went there with a chip on her shoulder. It was during her idle hours that she got to feeling so discontent. She tried a hobby or two but nothing satisfied her. She took up sewing, but since we went out so seldom the need for clothes wasn't great. Of course she had her flowers and her garden, but they were small compared to others and didn't take up a great deal of her time. I guess it was during these lonely hours that she began to think so much about New York and the good times there. She was getting more restless all the time and began to talk of another change."

Margie's change of mind did not come suddenly nor without some effort to avoid it. The change came a little at a time each day as the situation grew worse.

"Margie's resentment of her whole unpleasant living schedule was finally aimed at me. She complained of my night job and of our never getting to go anywhere. What was bothering her was that we were not able to go into the big city and have some of the fast night life she was accustomed to. But I was responsible for the trouble as well as she. I was content to do my work and stay around the house playing with Billy. I had grown up in rather quiet surroundings and didn't miss the gay times at the night club at all. It was selfishness on my part too. I was doing what I wanted to do and didn't care what others did. But that wasn't making our home a happy one."

Life became more unbearable for Margie with each passing week. She felt that she was couped up and she became even more restless and discontent. She began grumbling about almost everything and very often took out her neurotic-spite on Billy with heavier than necessary spankings.

"Margie expected more out of life than this and she felt that she was being cheated. Again and again she told me she wanted to have fun while she was still young, but I thought it was time she settled down and became an adult. Then she wanted to go to work for relief of her everyday drudgery. She wanted to put Billy in a day-nursery but I wouldn't hear to that at all. I knew what it was like to be left in the care of others and I didn't want my son to share the same experience. But this difference of opinion led to serious trouble. She didn't think I was being fair and she told me so."

"Look Roger, I don't care anything about your past. All I'm

concerned with right now is keeping myself from going crazy. You don't know what its like, staying around this place twenty-four hours every day week in and week out. I want some variety. I want to go some place and do something different. But you can't understand. You're happy. You've got a change everyday down at the office. You see new people and do different things on the job. But with me its different. I do the same old thing all the time and I'm tired of it—sick and tired of it. And I warn you, I'm going to take only so much of this and then I'm going to blow my lid. Just don't push me too far. I don't like this setup one bit and I'm liable to change it most any time."

But Roger was firm and this developed into a case of the irresistible force meeting the immovable object. Neither would budge, out of spite. So instead of the quarrels eventually dying down they increased in intensity.

"Roger, I'm warning you, I'm not going to take much more of this! Either you're going to make some kind of change so our family can be together more and go places together or I'm going to do something you won't like."

"I didn't believe Margie would do anything really rash so I stood my ground. I was too satisfied with things as they were to change them. I thought she was just taking the adjustment to small-town life hard and would soon be over it. I had everything I wanted in life; a wife, a son, a good job and future security. But I failed to figure one angle—our church life."

Conditions between Margie and Roger grew steadily worse. Roger kept thinking that she would finally settle down while Margie believed more and more that her husband was abusing her intentionally.

"Things got so bad that I started hating to go home after work. Margie no longer met me at the door with an embrace and a kiss. She was usually off in some other part of the house sulking and thinking of more hateful things to say to me. Our home which once sheltered our love was now only a frame covering our antagonism and growing hatred."

In one last desperate effort Roger tried to reason with Margie.

119

"Please be sensible! You're a grown woman now! You have a child to take care of. Surely you can find something to occupy your time. Besides, you know I can't run off to the city every time you feel like it. But we'll try to go more often. I'll try to get a day off once in awhile and we can enjoy ourselves."

"No Roger, that's not enough. I'm disgusted with all your fancy schemes. You're all talk and no do. I want a change. I'm even willing to leave Westvalley. Let's go west. I don't care what, but let's do something. I'm losing my mind in this motheaten burg. Now make up your mind, are we going to make some changes or are we not? If we're not I'm going to pack up my things and get out of here. I hate it here and I'm not going to stay here any longer!"

"When I realized how serious our rift was it was too late to correct it. I promised to ask for my old day work back and to be with the family more. But I could tell it was no use— something inside Margie had broken. She didn't plan to stay in Westvalley any longer and yet I couldn't see how we could just pick up everything all of a sudden and move. It was a hard decision to make and I guess I made the wrong one. But a thing or two that she said made me furious."

"Alright, alright, that's enough. You can call me spineless and helpless if you want to, but just don't call me nogood. Don't ever call me that! I'm as good as you or anybody else in this world, and don't you forget it! But if you think I'm so nogood then pack up your stuff and get on back to your mother. I don't think you're any good either—at least you're not any good for me."

CHAPTER 9

A DIVIDED HOUSE

" 'A HOUSE DIVIDED against itself cannot stand.' How often have I heard that, only to give it slight notice and then promptly forget it. This old axiom came home to me though when I began to see the foundations of our home crumbling under the strain of constant bickering. It was Margie's failure to make the adjustment to our new living situation combined with my stubbornness that broke our home. I tried to reason with her but she always had some kind of comeback."

"Roger, you're the coldest, hard-hearted, bull-headed person I ever knew. You couldn't see a point if a person drew you a picture of it on paper. I'm telling you if you don't give in somewhere we won't be together long. Its not fair to me and its not fair to Billy. You're only thinking about your selfish self. All you want is what will make you happy. But the day will come when you'll think about my wishes more. Just you wait and see."

"Now look Margie, you've got to grow up! After all you're not in high school now. You've got to get hold of yourself and act like a grown-up woman. My change in hours should come on through before too long and things will be different then. And we'll go places too."

These words were falling on deaf ears, for Margie had been laying her plans for leaving Roger for some time. After her mind was made up she quit nagging and her fault-finding dropped to a minimum. She just didn't care any longer.

"By this time word was all over town that the Scott feud was reaching its climax. Some people in Westvalley shook their heads when they saw us in town. They seemed sympathetic and I appreciated their interest but Margie ignored them all.

I guess others found our spats a source of juicy gossip. But we didn't pay the gossips much mind, we didn't think they counted."

The people of Westvalley were greatly concerned about the condition of the Scott home. Much of the concern was unfounded in that it was based on idle rumor. Some had already decided that Margie was not fit to care for Billy. They had heard that she beat the child without mercy. Others took her side against Roger and contended that he was too stern and was incompetent as a father. The mentality of both parties was questioned by some, but definite conclusions about the situation were seldom reached. This was just the usual talk that goes on in a small town.

"Margie and I were both to blame for not having close friends to help us during these troublesome days. We didn't go anywhere much and didn't see anyone often. We just didn't feel the need I guess, at least I didn't. I had all I wanted and didn't want anything to change it. Change—perhaps that was the thing I was fighting most. I had everything to my liking and I was afraid that a change in any way would tear down my happiness. I tried several last-minute compromises with Margie when she told me she was definitely going to leave me, but they were not enough. I guess she saw through my offers. I was willing to give a little, but never agreed to a real adjustment of our living schedule. Maybe that's why Margie hurt me so before she left."

"I absolutely refuse to remain in this God-forsaken town any longer! I married you thinking that I would have a good home and a good time, but look what a mess you've made of it! I haven't asked you for anything that any other wife wouldn't feel justified in asking. But do you listen? No sir, not for one minute! I'm sick of this place and of you and those smug people downtown. I guess they're enjoying our squabbles. Well, let them go ahead and enjoy them; somebody ought to. I know I'm not."

Roger tried to ease up a bit and listen to Margie's reasoning more, but when her temper flared his did too. And the more they talked the more stubborn he became.

"Alright, what will you gain if you leave me? You'd have

to work for your own living and that won't be very soft. Don't forget it. You've always had it soft. Maybe that's what's wrong with you, you just haven't grown up yet. But you will someday."

"You've said enough Roger! When you say things like that I boil inside. And of all people to be saying such things—you're the *least* qualified. You think I'm bluffing about leaving. Well I'll admit that at first I didn't really mean it, at least I didn't think I did, but now my mind's made up. I'm going to leave you here to rot in this dump. And this time I'm not kidding!"

The next morning Roger came in from work to find Margie's and Billy's clothes packed. At first this startled him, but then he decided to call her bluff.

"So, you're running away. You're not big enough to stay and work your problems out. Even Billy's smarter than that. Aren't you son? You wouldn't leave daddy would you? And mother can't do it either and be happy."

With those last words Margie exploded. "Listen to me Mr. Scott, I couldn't stay here now if my life depended on it. Why I couldn't be happy with you if we lived on the moon, and what's more I wouldn't try to. I hate you. Just like you hate me. Now would you mind getting my bags down to the station or do I have to call a taxi? We're leaving on No. 19 at 10:00."

"My pride was still pretty high so I agreed to carry the luggage to the station, but I fussed all the way down. Margie tried to calm me down but I didn't calm."

"The least you can do is get rid of us quietly, Roger. Look at all those people peering out of their windows. Now I wish we'd called the taxi."

"The rest will do you good and Billy will enjoy a little stay with his grandparents. Yes sir, if there's anything I can't stand its a nagging woman—and lately you've been the world's worse. It'll be nice to have a little peace and quiet around the house for a change. Yes sir, that will be different, wont it?"

Margie was getting angry again. She had tried to be civil and hold her tongue on their last day together, but with Roger she found this impossible.

"It'll be a hot day in Alaska when you see me coming back Mr. Know-it-all! I've had all of you I can stand and more. If I'd known you in Centerville like I know you now I would never have married you! You're about the sorriest speciman of a husband I know of. You disgust me."

"This must have been a funny sight to those who didn't know the seriousness of the situation. There I was stomping down to the depot with a suitcase under each arm and just a talking. I was so angry that I didn't even speak politely to those we met along the way."

At the station Roger kissed Billy goodbye and told Margie to get her rest and hurry back home. Billy cried for his daddy and when Margie's back was turned he ran back into the vestibule of the coach and tried to get off the train.

"I didn't pay much attention to the train as it left Westvalley. I thought Margie and Billy were gone for a week or so, but no more. The thought that this might be the end had never received serious consideration. My philosophy had often been that with a little luck I would have a model home. And even though things didn't look too bright at the moment I never felt that our trouble was more than a lover's quarrel."

Roger had been a lonely child most of his early years. He thought he knew real loneliness, but that was a thing of the past. For a week or so he enjoyed the quietness about the house and the relief from their past warfare. But when days turned into weeks and the weeks into a month, and then two months, a fear arose in his heart. For the first time he wondered if maybe Margie was not bluffing after all.

"During the second month of our separation I began to realize that Margie wasn't coming back, or at least as soon as I had expected. Westvalley was already turning into a ghost-town for me. There was no one there that I cared about. We had made few friends and no close ones so I was left out in the cold. Then when I was more convinced that my home wasn't going to be restored I lost interest in everything. Now I was only a shell of a man. My heart had left Westvalley with Margie's and Billy's love, and my happiness was slowly dying."

Letters came from Margie occasionally. However, they were

too far apart to suit Roger. He wanted a letter everyday and felt that he was entitled to them, but he did well to get one a week.

"Though the letters were slow in coming they did keep me informed about Billy. Margie told me that her folks had moved back to New York and that they had redecorated their home. She and Billy were living with them and she was working at a large downtown department store.

"The days were long as well as the nights with Margie and Billy gone. I continued to work on my night shift and got my sleep in the day time. However, I seldom slept over five hours a day, and sometimes not that much. I had too much on my mind. At first the neighbors invited me over to meals with them, but I thought they were just pitying me so I refused. I didn't want anyone to pity me. I had my pride. The preachers in town came by and offered to help me patch up my rift with Margie but I refused their help too. I figured what I couldn't straighten out myself could just stay unstraightened. I had my pride to think of."

The weeks dragged into months and Roger continued to refuse help of any kind. And instead of his loneliness getting better it got worse. In his refusal of material and spiritual help he cut himself off socially in the town. He had no close friends and had killed his chances of making any now.

"I thought I'd get used to living alone but I soon saw that I never would. No one can know the joys of companionship with a wife and child and then throw them overboard and not be hurt deeply. I missed the family gatherings at meals and Billy's little war whoops when I got home from work. The hours of fun we had together in the garden and in the yard were gone too. No more croquet games or walks out into the country to relax the mind and to get close to Nature. I had learned too late and the hard way. I was sorry now for all the misery I had caused Margie and myself. I was thinking clearly again."

When Roger fully realized that Margie was gone he dropped to lower depths of despair.

"I had thought that nothing could be as bad as those days

when I felt unwanted in Centerville. I thought I was friendless then, but this isolation was even worse. It was tearing my heart out to think that I had lost Margie and Billy forever."

Roger finally swallowed his pride and without hesitation wrote a long letter of apology to Margie. He appealed to her to bring Billy and come home. He admitted all the many mistakes he had made and promised to rearrange their life to make it more suitable to her.

"My pleas were rewarded with deathly silence. Letters were coming slowly enough up until now, but now they didn't come at all. The long hours of waiting were agonizing. I even left special instructions at the post office for the clerk to call me the moment I got a letter from New York. But none came, so I wrote another. I begged her to come back. I appealed to her better judgment by explaining Billy's need of both parents, but she did not reply. Every day I waited impatiently for the mail and rushed to the post office when I thought it had had time to be processed. But still no letter."

One day Roger's telephone rang after he had gone to sleep. A letter addressed to him had been overlooked during mail distribution at the post office.

"I rushed back into my bedroom and dressed as fast as I could and darted out of the house on a dead run. When I got to the mail window I could see the letter waiting for me there. It was from New York and I was hopeful. I even said a little prayer. But the news was bad. Margie said they were comfortably situated and that Billy was adjusting himself to his new life just fine. This letter hurt me deep inside. I wondered now if even Billy had quit loving me. No one seemed to want me now"

Just hearing from Margie was a good tonic for Roger even though the news was not good. The fact that she would still write him boosted his morale. This caused him to feel that there was yet a thread of hope that he might put his home back together again.

"Two weeks after I received Margie's discouraging letter I was visited by one of the officials of the company. He stopped by my desk and asked me to drop into his office for a confidential talk after working hours. Of course I went in after work. We talked about an hour and a half."

When the secret conference was over Roger left the office with a grim look on his face. He had promised the official that he would do his best to comply with his wishes. Then he hurried home and packed his bags. He returned to the station shortly and caught the 8:30 train to New York.

"The trip to New York wasn't too long for me since I was weary and slept most of the way. I was exhausted from months of loneliness and worry. So when I got this chance to relax I took advantage of it. At least I had something definite in mind now, something that might bring Margie back to our home in Westvalley. This new hope erased my former uncertainty and skepticism about my future life. It put new confidence in me and I felt better than I had in months."

Roger went directly to the Scofield's home when he arrived in New York. Billy was already in bed, but the Scofields awoke him to see his father. Later Margie came in from a late show. She appeared surprised to see Roger at first and a bit shaken, but she quickly recovered and treated her husband cooly.

"Margie and I made a date for the next afternoon to go out to dinner and talk about the new developments back at Westvalley. Then we all went to bed. It was very good to be in the house again with my own wife and son. The next morning Margie left for work with her father and I stayed at the house and talked with Mrs. Scofield and played with Billy. Margie's mother agreed with the decision of the railroad officials about the future of my job, but I still wasn't sure. With that out of the way I took Billy over to Central Park where we spent the day sightseeing and feeding pop corn and peanuts to the ducks and pigeons. On the way home we stopped by the store and I bought Billy everything in sight he wanted. Just being with my son again was soothing medicine for my burning heart."

The Scofields let Roger drive their car for the evening and he and Margie went out to dinner at one of the little spaghetti houses they had visited on their honeymoon. It was Roger's choice, not Margie's. Then after dinner they drove to the park and talked for hours.

127

"Look Margie, the Company says there's going to be a war in a few months. Everyone in the business is getting ready for it. As a matter of fact they've been expecting it for some time. That's why they put that ad in the *New York Times*. They wanted young men to handle the tough jobs during war time. The railroads are building all the new box cars and engines possible. They're gearing all their men and machines to meet the war effort."

Roger's attempts to penetrate the thick icy wall between him and Margie were noble, but to no avail for some time. However, she finally relented a little.

"But I don't see where this war will have anything to do with us. You can work for the railroad and I can keep my job here. That's simple enough. I like it that way. So why should we change it?"

"No, no, you don't understand. I can't stay there and you here and everything work out just fine. That's the catch! my draft status in Westvalley will be changed if my wife isn't living with me. You know how the folks there feel. They're very patriotic and those men on the draft board will make me 1-A pretty soon, unless my family is there."

"Then you need me and Billy to keep you out of the army, is that it?"

"No that's not it. I want you home for myself, but this new situation gave me the excuse to come here to see you. Darling, I'm sorry for all I did to you. I've repented a thousand times. Isn't there something I can do to make it up to you? Won't you let me try? Honest, I've learned my lesson. I need you and Billy more than anything else in the world. Yes—more than anything else in the world!"

"Then you mean you will stay on the job longer if Billy and I go back to Westvalley?"

"That's right. The officials have asked all of us fellows who are having trouble with our wives to get our domestic affairs straightened out. That way the draft board wont hurt the company's personnel by drafting them into the service at critical times. With you home I will be put on the list of men with jobs which are vital to the war effort. But if you don't come back

128

I'm a dead duck. They'll label me nonessential and send me right in."

Margie relaxed a little more in Roger's presence now and acted more friendly. They talked about the matter until two in the morning, but she would not make a decision. She was still afraid that enough scars of their marriage had not healed. With due caution she asked for time to think on the matter more. She wanted to see how she and Roger would get along while being together a few days again. Down deep she was afraid that if she went back with her husband only renewed quarreling and heartaches would follow.

"Margie asked me to telegraph for an extension of time so we could talk about the matter some more. I did this of course and got the extension. Then the next afternoon we met again and visited some of the night spots in New York. She seemed perfectly at ease and at home in those places. It was quite evident that this was the life she had missed so much at West-valley. She missed it so much that she was willing to break up her home to come back to it. I had no idea whether she had been dating other fellows since she returned home, nor did I ask her about it. I thought it would be hard enough to get her to come back to Westvalley with me without starting new fights. But I felt fairly safe in concluding that she had several different escorts taking her around to the various clubs."

While Roger was talking on the last night of his stay in New York Margie was thinking. She admitted to herself that she never thought of losing Roger to another woman, but she had not considered this new angle. Machine gun bullets, bombs and enemy snipers could take him away from her. Then the thought of losing her husband did stir an emotion deep in her heart. Then she knew. In spite of the very bitter resentment she felt toward Roger and the many grudges she had been holding against him she did still love him, some at least. Still, she was careful not to commit herself. She had been hurt once and wanted to avoid the horrible experience again.

Roger felt that he must return to work the next day so he made one last appeal.

"Well Margie, I'm going to take the next train back home

in the morning. I believe I've said all I can. It looks like I'll have to go into the service sooner or later. You'll decide the time. But knowing that I will, I'm begging you to come back with me and let me have a happy life a little while longer. I need you and Billy at home and I believe you want your own home. Really honey, I've never stopped loving you for one moment. We were just young crazy kids and we hadn't learned to give and take. But I've learned my lesson now and I think I know better how to be a good husband. Things will be different this time. I know they will because I'm willing to do anything to see that they are."

"But Roger, I'm not sure. I'm just not sure at all. It might work out and it might not. We thought our marriage was the perfect one to begin with. I'm afraid to go through another nightmare like we've been through. I know I'd go crazy. So you see I just don't know what to say. Maybe I need more time to think it over, I just don't know for sure. Give me more time to think."

The next morning Roger packed his things and Margie drove him to the station.

"Goodbye darling, I'll be waiting for your answer. I need you and Billy and I can't ever be happy again without you. Maybe our spats were good for us in spite of the wounds. At least they proved to me that I love you more than anything else in the world. My life has been a long, miserable existence without you. Please consider coming home soon. I may have only a short time at the most and I want to spend that time with you and Billy. Well, here's my train. Please decide real soon and let me know. I'll not rest easy again until I hear from you."

Chapter 10

WAR CLOUDS

"Margie took a few more days to think the matter over. Then she wrote me that she would give her boss at the store two weeks notice and then I could expect her home. It was a happy day for me when she and Billy arrived back at our little house on Landsford street. Most of our bitter feelings were gone now and Margie's resentment of me was not evident. I had done everything possible to make their return home as pleasant as possible and in turn she pitched in to get things back like they were before we separated."

Billy was overjoyed when he returned to his home and to his own private room. He was a bigger boy now and tried to help keep his room to some extent. Now he had a yard to play in, whereas he had none in New York. Neither were the children as rough to play with here as those in the big city. Billy was happy to be home again and Margie felt some relief in being free to run her own house. Roger was bubbling over with enthusiasm.

"Margie, I've already swung the deal! I'll be back on day work the first of the month. I told the boss that was one of the conditions of my staying with the company. It wasn't nearly as hard getting the change as I had expected. Now we can profit by our past mistakes and make a real life for each other and for Billy. And we'll have fun too. Just you wait and see, you're going to be glad you came back to Westvalley."

Within a few days the Scotts were settled in their home again and were making adjustments to their new life together. Both had aged considerably in experience and emotions. They had suffered through some of the bitterest feelings of which the human race is capable. Both had failed to live up to the sacred vows they had committed themselves to in their wedding and they had paid the bitter and horrible penalty.

"Everything was running along just fine with us after this. I went out of my way to please Margie and she responded to my wishes without a word. Perhaps we overdid it at first, but both of us were anxious to avoid even the slightest friction arising between us. We were learning to give and take now as married couples should, and as we should have in the first place. We were just happy that we had learned our lesson while our home was still in condition to be repaired."

The Scotts were at ease in their home now and were reconstructing a homelife far superior to their former situation. But one thing kept them from being totally confident of their future together. War clouds kept appearing over the horizon of international affairs. And the closer the war got to the United States the sooner Margie felt that she would have to give up her husband to the armed forces.

"It was Sunday, December 7th, when Margie and Billy and I were seated at the breakfast table and were talking about our future. We couldn't seem to get the subject off our minds. Everyone else was getting that unsettled feeling and we were feeling its effects too. We mentioned a lot of what-ifs and in-cases and all, but decided that come what may, we would always stand by each other. We talked about the same way at noon. Then it was about 1:30 when we were all in Billy's room making animal figures out of his molding clay. The radio was on and some of our favorite music was playing when the station announcer interrupted the program.

"We interrupt this program to bring you an emergency news bulletin. Airplanes from the Japanese Pacific Fleet attacked the United States fortifications at Pearl Harbor this morning. Many ships in the harbor have been sunk or damaged. The airfields have been bombed and machine-gunned. Many American airplanes were destroyed in the surprise raid and other attacks are expected at any moment. Casualties among the civilians and military personnel are believed to be high. Keep tuned to this station for further details. We return you to the program now in progress."

132

"Margie and I sat there stunned. We had been expecting the news of war, but had not dreamed that our nation would be stabbed in the back like this. It was hard to believe because we had just read in the morning paper that a Japanese envoy was in Washington to discuss America's differences with Japan. But it all became clear. While we were talking peace in Washington we would be off guard and that made it easy for the Japanese Air Force to catch our defenses napping."

The United States struck back at the Japanese forces as rapidly as she could reorganize their battered forces at Pearl Harbor. And the country as a whole was aghast at this sudden attack upon its unsuspecting installations in the Pacific. Though the radio announcement was a shock to many in the country, it did not find everyone unprepared. The world had already been conditioned to war through the bloody revolution in Spain a few years earlier and also by the Japanese attack on Manchuria. Italy had also been fighting the little country of Ethiopia and England and France had been at war with imperialistic Germany for several years. Though the United States tried to remain neutral, it had become more evident all the time that such a course was impossible. Most everyone expected a global conflict sooner or later and they knew when it did come it would affect every man, woman and child in the world. Now it was here. World War II had begun.

"By the first of the year I was routing three times as many trains through our yards as before. American boys were leaving the country and the cities and towns by the hundreds of thousands and were passing through our yards on the way to the Pacific coast. We got reports every day that more and more were boarding ships and were entering the theater of operations. Patriotic feeling in our office was running high and we felt it also in town. The radios were going day and night urging young men to get into the service of their country. This made me feel that I should enlist right away in spite of my family, but the bosses reminded me that I had been trained to serve the war effort in the office."

But as the war grew in intensity and the enemy continued to inflict great losses on the American divisions in the Pacific,

Roger felt the urge to quit his job anyway and go into military service immediately.

"I hadn't been taught about war from the Christian standpoint so I was eager to get in there and kill as many men as I could. I felt that the more dead Japanese and Germans there were, the sooner the war would be over. But each time I got restless and asked for permission to quit, the district supervisor reminded me that I was frozen on my job and could not quit."

"We've got to keep these engines running on time, son. These materials and men must get to the coast at the earliest possible time. The work you're doing is as important as shooting on the front lines because you're getting their guns and ammunition to them. Look at that load of tanks on those flatcars there. Those boys in the islands need those tanks and they need them now. And they need food and medical supplies too. Look at that troop train yonder. See next to the last car? That's carrying nothing but medicine. Now look at these charts. See thousands and thousands of miles of rails? Well these are the arteries of supply to the ships on the coast. And its as important to get men and supplies to the battle areas as it is to be there yourself. Remember we've trained you to do that. If you leave us now your going will cripple our work for awhile and that's defeating our purpose. And just remember that carrying a rifle isn't the only way to fight a war. Your time will come soon enough anyway. The company orders are that every man should stay on his job until the local draft board decides that they've got to have him. You're a part of essential industry, so sit tight until you hear from the board."

"This procedure quieted me down temporarily each time, but I never settled back to my work completely satisfied. I didn't feel that I was doing enough. Other boys were overseas getting killed and here I was sitting at the controls guiding trains through our switches. Day after day the troop trains came through on the way to the coast and I watched them, grim faced and determined. They were going into action and I felt that I should go alongside them. I was happy with my home and job right now, but everyone else was doing it and I wanted to go along."

134

A year drug by and Roger continued to suffer from constant mental unrest. His happy home compensated some for his having to stay behind, but even that didn't settle his mind. And at this time the American forces were taking a terrific beating in the islands and were withdrawing in many of the campaigns. Such news tended to keep Roger's blood pressure high.

"Finally my reclassification came. I got a card from the local board and it had a 1-A on it. Then I knew that my time was short. This meant that I might have sixty more days at home at the most and fifteen days at the least. Margie and I broke the news to Billy as gently as we could. We wanted him to get used to the idea so it wouldn't upset him like our separation had before. But Billy didn't understand. He knew that things were alright between his mother and me now, so he saw no reason for us parting. He was playing again as usual. But he picked up interest when everything suddenly quieted down. Then he knew something was about to happen."

Greetings from the Government arrived one morning while Margie was tending the flowers in the front yard. She noticed that the envelope was from the United States War Department. She rushed to the telephone and called Roger to come home at once. He was in town shopping and stopped in the middle of a purchase and rushed home.

"It was a relief to both of us in one respect. The suspense had been growing every day and it was getting worse. I guess both of us feared another separation but neither would let on such to the other. I was instructed to report to the nearest induction center. We knew that time was short now so we stayed together all we could. Margie was very sweet and did everything possible to give me a beautiful last week to remember. Of course we went out a lot and tried to be as gay as possible. We reminded ourselves that thousands of other couples were going through this same thing. The thought was comforting, but we were suffering just the same."

A woman arrived in Westvalley to take over Roger's job. She had been training several days when Roger got his final notice. Another man took over her training program and let him have all of his remaining time with his family.

"Margie and I did a lot of talking those last few wonderful days. We made plans about her getting a job in town while I was gone and about her keeping the house so I would have a home to come back to. We vowed to each other that we wouldn't change either. We'd promised to keep on loving each other no matter how long we were apart. These talks strengthened us and made my leaving much easier. We had put our home together again and both of us desperately wanted to keep it that way."

Roger went to the depot alone the next morning. He chose to leave the family at the house, thinking that it would be easier on all of them.

"Goodbye my darling, and I'll be thinking of you every minute. We'll get this war over with as soon as possible and get back home to our normal living again. Don't forget to write and I'll write you every day too."

"Goodbye Billy. Now you're the boss-man around the house while daddy's gone. You feed the puppy like a big man and keep the rabbits watered and help mother in every way you can. You do things for mother just like you did for me and you mind real good too. I'll be sending you toys and souvenirs, so you be a good boy."

"God bless you sweetheart and don't forget to remember me in your prayers each night with Billy. We're both going to need them."

With this Roger kissed Billy and then Margie and abruptly left the house and walked downtown to the depot, all the while rubbing his tears on his sleeves. Billy didn't understand why his daddy was crying.

"From Westvalley I went on the train to the induction center. After several days of tests I went into the Marine Corps. Then as soon as we were sworn in we were joined by a group of other inductees and all of us were assigned to a troop train. All the men on this train were Marine personnel assigned to Paris Island, South Carolina for boot camp training. We started out one morning about ten o'clock and picked up more men all the way to the camp."

After many jolting stops and starts Roger's train drew to a final halt on a siding near the big Marine training center.

"We were herded into long cattle trucks and driven at breakneck speed over ten miles of the roughest terrain in the world. Most of us were exhausted at the end of the ride from fear and fatigue. Later we found out that this was the first of many initiations for raw recruits."

None of these new Marines looked like heroes that day. They lost their hair the first thing at the base barber shop and then they were inspected for bugs. Each man was stripped of his civilian clothes and was thoroughly de-loused, much to the embarrassment of some. Whether a man was suspected of carrying lice or not he got the treatment. A few of them got indignant about it but the majority made light of the fumigation episode and took it with a chuckle.

"Each of us was issued the usual military articles. I got a bundle of clothing and a bucket of soapy water. From then on everything was strictly military. When we weren't appearing for roll call we were in our barracks cleaning up or reporting for drill. They didn't even give me a choice of color when they issued my fatigues. Then when we finally got our nap and our haversack and our pair of boon-dockers, our equipment was complete."

Boot camp life had its ups and downs for Roger. After roll call and calisthentics came drill and marching.

"Most of my spare time was spent in rubbing my swollen feet and writing letters to Margie. And when I wasn't doing that I was cleaning my rifle or studying a manual telling how to care for it. My rifle wasn't heavy at all to begin with but after carrying it a few days it began to take on weight. But everything wasn't marching and saluting at Paris Island. We attended lectures and studied sanitation as well as military camouflage. For additional exercise we studied ju-jitsu and boxing, and practiced tumbling in the gym."

Roger's last two weeks at boot camp were spent on the rifle range.

"The first day or two they taught us how to fall, as if full-grown men didn't know how to fall down. They taught us to fall behind obstacles to protect us from enemy bullets and how to fall in firing position if the enemy was rushing us. Then we learned to roll down a hill if we made too good a target on our feet. We took this part of our training very seriously. We had joked a lot about our training at first but when we started crawling under barbed wire entanglements with live machinegun bullets whizzing over our heads we sobered up. We realized from this kind of practice that we were going to face an enemy who knew all the tricks of the trade. We knew too that if we came home at all it would be because we had mastered the skills of self-defense. All the fellows wanted to come home. Many of them had Margies and Billys who were looking for them."

Roger's group finished its training and was sent to San Diego. They were given only a few hours of liberty and then were put aboard waiting battleships and steamed out to sea.

"I barely had time to call Margie long-distance before we left. They were short of men in the Pacific and were moving new men over there as fast as possible. Some of my buddies and I were stationed aboard a battleship to stand guard. We were getting into the fight at a very critical time and we could tell that they were sending every man, plane and ship available into the firing lines."

It was late at night when the big battle-wagon slipped out of the harbor.

"I was on guard duty at the time and I sure got to feeling queer as those lights on the shore got smaller and smaller. I had never been away from my country before and I sure felt lost when those lights faded out. After this it was one battle after another with seasickness. The ship rolled and tossed and bounced in the waves and was especially bad when the winds were strong. I did everything I could think of to ward off the seasickness but nothing helped. I was sick every day we were on the water and nothing helped."

The battleship was headed in the direction of Pearl Harbor but only a few men in the chartroom knew it. They zigzagged the ship's course part of the time when submarine reports were made. It was Roger's duty to check the ship at night and make sure all lights were either out or completely concealed.

"A few days later the boys on the ship got awfully excited. They acted as though they had never seen land before. One of my buddies told me they could see old Diamond Head mountain near Pearl Harbor but I wasn't interested. Each day I had gotten weaker until I was finally confined to my quarters below deck. I had also taken a burning fever and complications had set in, so I didn't participate in the excitement on deck."

The huge ship slipped cautiously into Pearl Harbor. She edged past the damaged and sunk American fleet there. The battleship "Oklahoma" was on her side and close by was the bomb-shattered "Arizona" the men on board looked in amazement at the damage the sneak attack had done to a once-proud fleet of ships.

Eventually the battleship worked its way into the harbor proper and into full view of Honolulu and Waikiki beach. The green-horn sailors on board were disappointed because the docks were not full of grass-skirted hula dancers and a Hawaiian orchestra. Instead, the wharfs were teeming with halfclad and sweating natives who were moving supplies off the ships. This was wartime and everything was serious business at Pearl Harbor.

"My boat was to stay in port for three days while it refueled and took on ammunition, then it was scheduled to go into the battle zone. They took me to the base hospital for observation and treatment. The ship left in three days according to schedule but I wasn't aware of it. My fever had risen so high that I was delirious. I was so sick I didn't know anything— and didn't care."

Chapter 11

RUMORS FROM THE STATES

"My fever was running high every day now and when it went over 103° several time the doctors put me on the critical list. They tried every diagnosis they knew from jungle fever to tularemia. Finally they decided I had undulant fever. It was a bacterial disease which was accompanied by profuse perspiration and pain as well as swelling of the joints. They told me an enlarged spleen was also a usual symptom. When I asked them how I got it they explained that it was transmitted through milk. The other soldiers called my trouble Mediterranean fever. The doctors also told me that I would have a long and hard battle getting rid of my trouble; that I should remain as quiet as possible and be patient."

Roger had been confined to his bed several weeks when a nurse brought him his first mail from the States. It was a letter from Grandma Horton. She had written him all through boot camp and now was the first to cheer him up at Pearl Harbor. He had noticed lately that he had gotten two letters from her to every one from Margie, but he didn't pay it much mind. But when Grandma Horton brought up the same thought in her letter he began to wonder.

"Grandma was upset in her letter. I could tell by the way she wrote that she was nervous. The lines were irregular and the words weren't smooth as usual. She asked me if Margie had been ill or something. She said she hadn't gotten any mail from her for some weeks and that was very unusual. She and Margie wrote often and traded news from my letters. Sometimes I wrote one something and forgot to tell the other. Then too, Grandma was concerned about a change in the postmark on Margie's letters. She said they were not coming from Westvalley but from the city thirty-five miles away. I did think it was strange that Margie hadn't written me about being in the city, but I dismissed the idea from my mind. Since I hadn't gotten a letter from her in weeks I didn't have any reason to suspect anything. I knew I'd be getting a letter soon and could tell something from it."

Perhaps it was good that Roger hadn't thought too much about the changed postmarks on Margie's letters to Grandma Horton. He was undergoing daily examinations and was taking medicine which made him extremely nervous.

"What I didn't know then was that Margie had moved to the city and quit writing Grandma shortly after that. She hadn't tried to conceal her move particularly but just didn't see any use writing any longer. She had made a change and didn't think it was anybody's business. She had quit her job in West-valley and let our house go. Then she moved to the city and took a better job in one of the offices there."

When Roger's illness was correctly diagnosed the doctors began a long series of treatments. Within a few days some progress was noted and the staff was pleased. His fever went down to 100° and the swelling in his arms and legs wasn't so great. This turn for the better was very encouraging so he was allowed to be outside part of each day.

"I enjoyed the short trips out to Waikiki beach where I could lounge around and sleep under the palm trees and breath the fresh sea air. And I enjoyed the scenery too. The ships in Uncle Sam's Pacific fleet entered the port nearby and left for the battle areas from there. Ships had always intrigued me since I was a landlubber. I had always wanted to satisfy my curiosity. It gave me a real thrill too when each new convoy came by, guarded by cruisers and destroyers. And occasionally I saw a battleship or an aircraft carrier cutting the water. These trips to the beach were very good for me in more ways than one. Among other things, it got my mind off myself and my troubles. My aches seemed to be less on sunshiny days when I could be out too."

Margie's first letter arrived about a week after Grandma Horton's. By then Roger had forgotten all about his grand-

141

mother's concern. So when he got the letter he almost forgot to look at the postmark.

"I read the letter through a time or two before I remembered to check the postmark. I still didn't think it meant anything so I just gave it a passing glance. But then I turned back and looked at it again: Sure enough, it wasn't from Westvalley. It had a Montgomery postmark and it caused me to wonder. After seeing this I opened the letter and reread it. This time I tried to read between the lines to see if anything was out of the ordinary. But it was much the same as usual. She told me all about Billy and little about herself. She didn't mention having moved however. I thought that was strange."

Margie's next two letter contained the identical postmark to the first, still she said nothing about being away from Westvalley. This began to seem very strange to Roger. She had promised not to leave home until he came back from the war, but she was already gone. He wondered what it meant.

"I tried to be real careful not to read things into her letters that weren't there, but this was hard. Strange things had happened and there was no explanation given for them. That's why my casual interest in the subject changed to wonder, and finally to deep concern. Something was going on and I wasn't being told about it. That was a form of dishonesty and nothing good is ever connected with lying. She knew something and wasn't telling me. I hated to doubt her, my own wife, but these unexplained things began to get on my nerves. I began to imagine some pretty bad things. I had heard all about those 'Dear John' letters so many fellows in the service were getting and I had also seen what it had done to some of them. It changed them from men into human wrecks. Some of the men went A W O L, a couple of them shot themselves and the rest either just boiled and did nothing about it or threatened to kill their wives when they got back. They didn't make very pretty pictures in their rage."

Roger wanted to be fair however, so he reconsidered his bitter feelings and put away his skepticism until he had more definite grounds. He even censured himself for thinking such thoughts about Margie now. They had made up and were very

142

happy when he left. He felt a little ashamed of himself too for letting his imagination run away with him like that.

"But my problems grew, rather than diminished. In spite of all I could do the idea that Margie wasn't being fair with me hounded me day and night. Sometimes during the night I would wake up begging her to come back to me as I had done many times in Westvalley. But there was nothing I could put my finger on yet. The uncertainty and suspense were hard for a sick man to stand. And each letter after that seemed more forced than the one before. This wasn't like my Margie at all. I didn't understand and it was unnerving me greatly."

The staff psychiatrists visited in Roger's room frequently after his records showed a turn for the worse. The doctors were alarmed at his sudden decline and the nurses began reporting very unusual behavior on Roger's part. They suspected wife-trouble from the States right off because they had seen so much of it. About a third of their patients in the infirmary were suffering unnecessarily because they had given up in their fight to get well. Their wives had left them and they didn't care about anything anymore.

"I couldn't tell this man what my trouble was. I didn't know myself. And it seemed silly to me to tell a doctor that I suspected my wife, when I had no real grounds to base my opinion. But I guess I didn't have to tell him. He could see doubt and uncertainty written all over my face. He looked at me with pity but that didn't help me much. It just made me feel even more helpless."

When the psychiatrist made his report to the medical staff it was a gloomy one. He reported that Roger was suffering from extreme mental and physical tension. He said he would be a bad neurotic case in a few more weeks if something wasn't done for him. But after hearing all the facts the other doctors had their doubts about winning this case.

"On his second visit the psychiatrist stayed for hours and we just talked. He got me started and I poured my heart out to him. It had been a long time since I had had a person who would sit down and listen to my troubles. We finally got to the bottom of my trouble. He suggested that I stop trying to hide my problem. He encouraged me to write to Margie right away and get the matter settled. His reasoning was correct. If there was something wrong I would do better knowing what it was. And if nothing was wrong I would be relieved to find it out."

Roger followed the advice of the doctor and cabled Margie immediately for clarification of their relationship. It seemed foolish to make such a request when he had so little concrete evidence, but he followed the advice of his friend against his better judgment.

"I wasn't long in getting a reply to this question. It came as both a shock and relief to me. At least I knew something definite and I could quit imagining all sorts of horrible things. Margie replied that she was trying to get a divorce. She gave no reasons for this sudden change of mind. She just asked me not to stand in her way. I was relieved to learn that Billy was doing just fine and would be well taken care of. She didn't say how my son could get along so well without his father's help, but that was her claim."

"After receiving this bad news I cabled Margie at once and asked for further details. I was later told that the doctor added a report of my condition to the wire and asked her to settle our differences at all cost. However, she didn't seem concerned about me or my condition at this time. Her air mail special-delivery letter came to the hospital four days later. She explained that she had thought our marriage over carefully and had decided that it would never work out. She asked that we quit now while we were apart. She thought it would be easier that way. But she didn't know what her plan was doing to me."

The doctors kept Roger in bed with great difficulty after he knew the true story. He knew that he did not have the full story yet, and he hoped that he might do something to prevent Margie's foolish plans from succeeding. He threatened to stow-away on the first ship headed for the States. Then he talked to visiting airmen and tried to get some of them to help him hide aboard one of their transport planes which was evacuating the sick and wounded from the Pacific area. Roger was determined to get home somehow and straighten out his family affairs.

"One night while the nurses were busy I slipped out of bed and hobbled over to my closet and tried to put on my clothes. I planned to get away that night, but I didn't realize how weak and sore my swollen legs were. Just one more step back to my bed and I wouldn't have made it. Everything went black and I fell across the foot of the bed. After that episode I obeyed the doctor's orders and lay quietly in bed. I was confused now. I didn't know whether to quit caring at all or keep thinking in hopes of working out some scheme yet. Then I lay there hour after hour breathing hard and sweating profusely. I was sick in body but I was a lot sicker in heart. My arms and legs hurt but nothing like the pain in the left side of my breast and the doctors didn't have a bottled medicine which could mend a broken heart. I was now losing the dearest things in life and there was nothing I could do to prevent it."

"During the lonely hours and days that followed I tried to figure out just why Margie changed her mind. I wondered if I had said something wrong in my letters. Or I thought she may have gotten restless again, but I couldn't imagine her divorcing me because she was just restless. There was more to it than that. Then I wondered if I had been as good a husband to her as I had thought. Maybe I had failed to impress her as a father to our son. It didn't make sense. I couldn't find an answer. Then I wondered if she was weaker in character than I had given her credit. I thought that another man might be the trouble. She hadn't looked at another fellow seriously since we were married, I was sure. Or was I? Then I was weary of thinking about it and picked up a magazine and tried to get my mind off my tangled problem."

The next day Roger scribbled another cablegram. In it he begged her to forget the divorce idea and hold everything until he could see her in person and talk the matter out. He reaffirmed his love and reassured her that everything would turn out fine once they were together again. Then he added a warning at the last. He told her that if another man was the reason for her request that he would never rest until he found them and got back what was his. In tears he reminded her that she and Billy belonged to him and to no other man on earth.

"Margie's response to this note was a determined one. She told me that she was still working on the divorce and that she just about had it fixed so that she could get it with or without my consent. She mentioned that she had connections. So her mind was made up and there was apparently nothing that could change it. She was determined to break up our home and she was listening to no one."

"As a last resort I wrote Margie that she could not get a real divorce. I told her she had no grounds. Then I explained that I could never consent to a divorce since it violated the teachings of the Bible and my conscience as well. I told her she couldn't scripturally divorce me unless I was guilty of unfaithfulness to her, and I denied ever having been guilty of adultery. Then I warned her that she would never have the right to remarry anyone even if she did get a civil divorce. But at this point I doubted that any of my convictions or pleas would do any good."

Roger had turned to the Bible too late! During his earlier days when he and Margie were happy together he might have taught her the Lord's law against illegal divorces. But he had never done that, nor had he encouraged her to attend church services or read their Bible at home. Now his opportunities had passed and he was losing his home because of it.

"Days and weeks went by after this and no reply came from Margie. I wrote her again and again but got no reply. All my communications were returned unopened. Only silence and an increased lonliness rewarded my continued efforts. Then I began to get weaker. I didn't care anymore. Night after night I hoped I wouldn't wake up the next morning. If only the death-angel had come and taken me away from all this I would have been grateful."

As Roger's condition grew worse the doctors became greatly alarmed. He had quit eating and wouldn't go out to the beach and didn't want visitors of any kind in his room. He was attempting to kill himself by starvation of body and soul.

"Grandma Horton's letters were the only source of comfort

to me now. She was wonderful to me during my ordeal. She knew that her letters were the only source of encouragement and she wrote often, sometimes two or three letters a day, but she was straining for things to tell me. I could tell that by her letters, but I appreciated her efforts anyway. At least one person in the world still loved me and that was the only hope I had left."

The doctors at the hospital decided to ship Roger back to California on the first ship which had room to take him. They knew that the distance between him and his loved ones was against him and they knew they could remedy that.

"It took the doctors several days to find passage for me back to the States but they finally succeeded. There was a small room available on a hospital ship and I was put in there and a 'quiet please' sign was hung on my door. I don't remember a thing about the trip back. I was sicker than ever on the rolling and tossing ship. Some of the time I was conscious and part of the time I wasn't. I never knew when I went to sleep whether I would wake up or not."

"When our ship docked at San Diego I took a little more interest in my surroundings. And when they transferred me to the base hospital I showed a slight improvement. And in a few days with better care and equipment I gained some strength and ate a little occasionally. Still I was skin and bone because I hadn't eaten anything the last few days in Hawaii and nothing on board the ship. I drank some fruit juice to wet my mouth and that was all. But now, with better care, my fever went down and I developed an appetite.

One lone letter came to the hospital for Roger each day. It was from Centerville and had Grandma Horton's handwriting on it each time. And the contents remained about the same, news about Centerville, but no word from Margie.

"One day the news was better. Grandma wrote me that she had received a short note from Margie requesting my current address. Grandma didn't know what to make of it but she sent my address to her immediately. She was in hopes that Margie was planning to come to San Diego and the suggestion aroused my hopes some."

Roger began to smile a little each day much to the encouragement of the hospital personnel who was in charge of his case. The ray of hope was a dim one, but it was there just the same. The reaction to Margie's request was remarkable in Roger. The doctors noticed it and the nurses talked about it. There was yet hope that a miracle would happen.

"I well knew that the day of miracles were over, but I dreamed and prayed for just a half-miracle. I prayed fervently and earnestly that God would bring my wife to see me. I didn't know where she was or what she was doing or who she was with, but I begged God to intervene in her life and bring her back to me."

Roger responded to the new treatments he was receiving at the San Diego hospital, but he was far from recovery yet. His limbs were still swollen and his fevers continued to sap his energy. At times his whole body grew numb and perspiration stood out on his face and arms for hours at a time. When it did he suffered untold pain. Then the fever would subside and he would relax again for awhile. Under these circumstances the only hope the doctors saw for Roger was to get his mind at ease. Whatever problems he had must be solved and to his satisfaction. Therefore the order went out that his wife was to be located at all costs. The chaplain of the hospital was put in charge of the effort. He in turn solicited the aid of the psychiatrists and the public relations men. They called the Red Cross and then the police. Calls went out everywhere including radio stations and newspaper stories. They had all the cities in the mid-west named Montgomery thoroughly checked, but still no signs of Margie. She had vanished and left no traces of her whereabouts.

"It wasn't until December that anything else happened to excite us. I was making some progress back to health and was just taking life as it came. I didn't know what I would do when I was well enough to get out of the hospital. I knew I would get a medical discharge, but after that I had no plans. And it was just as well that I didn't have plans because the telegram I got at the hospital would have changed them. It was a wire from Margie. When it arrived in the office a nurse was dispatched to my room with it immediately. Then the doctors and nurses waited outside the door to hear the good news. I tore the envelope apart hurriedly and then I read it."

148

"Pfc. Roger Scott
Marine Hospital
San Diego, California

Divorce granted yesterday Billy fine Sends love to daddy Sorry our marriage didn't work out Plan to marry Ben this month Take good care of yourself.

Margie."

"My hands began to tremble as I read line after line. The more I read the worse it hurt. I read it a second time. Then I read it a third and a fourth and still I couldn't believe it. I didn't *want* to believe it. I didn't think those words could be telling the truth. This couldn't be happening. But then the truth dawned on me. Human nature finally let the reality of it sink deep in my heart. This was the end. Somehow she had gotten her divorce. She told lies and misrepresented the facts, but still she got the divorce."

"After reading the telegram again I went over to the bed and fell across it sobbing aloud. This brought the doctors and nurses to my side. One of the doctors put his hand on my shoulder and said 'tough luck, son, tough luck.' "

"The presence of these people in my room irritated me. I wanted to be alone, so I jumped up from the bed and asked everyone out and when they didn't respond as quickly as I thought they should I screamed at them to leave me alone. Then I ran to the door and slammed it against them and stacked the table and chairs against it. I didn't want them coming back in to learn about my business. It was none of their affair and I didn't like them snooping."

Intense heat rushed into Roger's head and his blood raced through his body until his heart labored hard and his veins stood out blue against his reddened skin. His body grew moist with perspiration and a scowl came onto his face as he began to grit his teeth. Then he went to the bed and sat down upon its edge. His body began to weave like the angry lion at the zoo that wanted out of his cage. His head was swimming now and his vision blurred until nothing was visible to him. Different emotions swept through his heart. He feared and then turned to rage. Then he had an intense craving for revenge. Pride and jealousy combined to infuriate him and he began to beat his head with his fists in a mad fit. And finally his madness subsided and he began to reason about his plight.

"I was licked. For the first time I admitted to myself that I was whipped. I saw no hope now. There was nothing I could do. I had been beaten for some time but I was too stubborn to admit it. Until now I had never admitted to myself that Margie could ever quit loving me, but now I knew that she had. I was wrong—dead wrong all the time."

"My next problem was the future. But what future did I have to look forward to without Margie and Billy? What else did I have to live for? They were all I had, all I cared about. And now they were gone from me forever! Well, it was all over now. I had fought life and its complex problems and I had lost. My marriage had failed and my home was destroyed. How stupid I had been. I lost it all through ignorance and sin and indifference. I was selfish and narrow and it cost me all I had. Now I saw why. I had tried to make my way through life without God. I had left Him out and that caused me to fail."

More than an hour passed before Roger moved. Had the nurses seen him during that time they would have pitied him but also feared him. He had a wild look in his eyes and he snarled animal-like as he grumbled vindictive words against Margie and Ben. When his mind returned to thoughts of them his flesh went hot and then cold intermittently. His fever was rising to dangerous heights but he would not let anyone in the room to help him.

"Though I was bewildered and disorganized I was determined to do something drastic. I decided not to take this licking lying down. I was going to fight for what was mine, and I might even kill if anyone tried to stop me. I had my rights! Ben had taken advantage of me. While I was sick overseas, he courted my wife. And the more I thought about this Ben fellow the more enraged I became. The thoughts in my mind were savage, but I had settled on a way to stop Ben from taking what was mine. I'd stop him. I'd kill him!"

Roger calmed down after he got his plan well in mind. He moved the table and chairs from in front of the door and made like he was going to behave. It was time for supper so he straightened up his bed and waited for it. When it arrived he asked for extra helpings though he had no appetite at all. He knew he would need all the strength possible to carry out his scheme. When the nurse tried to take his temperature he begged off and got his way. He got by without the nurse learning of his turn for the worse.

"Midnight finally came and I slipped out of bed and dressed. Then when I heard the nurse pass my room I knew she would soon be around the corner on her regular room check. I rolled up the blankets from the closet and put them under my cover to make it look like I was still asleep. Then I opened the door into the hall and peered out. No one was in the hall or at the information desk so I slipped out and ran to the front door. Once outside I began to run hard."

"The cool, crisp air felt good to my aching lungs as I raced down the boulevard. I put up my thumb several times at passing cars but none of them stopped to give me a ride. So I ran when I felt like it and walked when I was too winded to go faster. I finally got to the city limits where the highway forked. I stopped here to read all the direction signs. It wasn't until then that I realized I didn't know where I was going. I took out the telegram and read it but it had been badly handled and the name of the sending point was missing. However the state was clearly Florida and the first letter of the city was O. I didn't know any cities in Florida beginning with O but I figured I could find it once I got to the state. This information gave me the general direction I wanted to go so I took the right hand turn and started trudging down the highway towards the east."

"I walked all night and well into the next day. A few cars passed me during the night but none of them stopped to give me a lift. I stopped along the way to rest some too, but not for long. I wanted to put all the distance between me and the Marine base I could. I didn't know how much time I might have to stop Margie's foolish plan to marry Ben, but I knew I must hurry."

"Late that afternoon I sighted a State Highway Patrol car and felt sure that they had heard the general alarm about my escaping from the hospital. I was AWOL from the marines as well as being absent from the hospital. I just knew these men were looking for me to take me back."

The patrol car did have a pick-up order on Roger, and they saw him when he darted off the road into the brush. This suspicious behavior caught their eye and they immediately gave chase.

"All that saved me was the head start I had. I ran through the woods and finally got over a hill and hid in the rocks. The patrolmen didn't find me but they nearly scared me to death. By now I was so nervous and upset that my mind began to blank out and play tricks on me. Even my vision came and went as the heat in my head grew more intense. I guess I went into a state of shock after that because I didn't remember a thing until the next day. When I woke up I wandered around in the woods hysterically for an hour. But finally I came to my senses and set down to get my directions straightened out."

"One thing I remember very vividly was that I felt sure now that the world was against me and was hunting me to harm me. I guess I hated everybody then. The thought kept recurring to me that they were trying to stop me from getting to Margie. But I was determined to show them. I was going to keep on running and hiding until I got to Florida. Then I planned to straighten things out. I knew Billy would be on my side and together I figured we could stop his mother's insane plan to marry another man."

"By this time the sun was shining brightly and it felt good to my chilled body. I got up and stretched my tight muscles and they hurt awfully bad. I screamed out a time or two as I straightened my bent body. When I felt like moving I slipped back out to the highway and started on my journey again. Numerous cars passed me but none paid me any mind or offered me a ride. I must have looked too dirty and ragged. But a few miles down the highway I found my ride. I came to some railroad tracks and knew a freight would come along sooner or later. When I got to the crossing I turned down the tracks and walked until I came to the bottom of an uphill grade. Then I hid back

152

off the right-of-way in the bushes until my ride should come along."

"After a couple of hours a long freight whistled at the crossing and started up the grade. When the cars were moving slow enough I climbed to the top of a dirt mound and jumped onto a flatcar as it passed by. Then I listened and looked to see if anyone had seen me. And after no one challenged me I got up and worked my way back to a cattle car where I could hide in the straw. I was very pleased with myself now. I was going to make some real time and for all I knew the train might be headed for Florida."

"But had I known at this point what lay ahead of me I would have jumped off that train and flagged down the first patrol car that came along and begged to be put in the Marine clink. Jail or anything else would have been better than what I was heading into at this time. I might have solved my problem in some other way, but I was too headstrong at this time to care what I was going to do."

The train rambled along mile after mile and Roger thought it was taking him closer to a solution to his worries, but in reality was taking him closer to the spot where he would commit his awful crime.

"When I went so long without food that I could stand it no longer I jumped from the train and began looking around. It was night time and I finally spotted a little country grocery store. The latch on the door wasn't hard to work and the lock was bad anyway so I got in easy. I ate all I wanted and then bundled up some cheese and crackers and took the grocer's money out of his wooden drawer. Also there was a revolver in the drawer so I took that too. I thought I might need one sometime."

"After I robbed the store I walked back down the train tracks until I came to another highway where I started trying to hitch a ride. It was raining now and cold. It was shortly after this that the lumberjacks picked me up and mistreated me and I killed them. Then I ran away and stayed at the Simmon's place until I decided to give myself up. The police took me back to town where I got some medical treatment and as soon as I was able they put me in jail to await my trial. Then my trial came of course. The jury listened intently to the gory details of my crime and finally went out to decide whether to set me free, give me life imprisonment or send me to the electric chair. When the jury returned to the courtroom they rendered a verdict of . . . . . .

●

Just then Roger's dream stopped abruptly. He jumped up from the hard wooden bench he had been sleeping on and looked around the room. He shook his head to clear his mind and then sat back down amazed that he could have dreamed his life so realisticly.

"It was the end of the dream that awakened me. Just as the jury foreman was about to read the jury's decision the dream stopped. Then I was curious what the decision would have been if I had slept just a few minutes longer. I got up then and went over to the door. The courtroom was silent. But faintly I could hear voices discussing my fate. The debate was still going on so I settled back on the bench to wait. I wondered what the verdict would be."

Chapter 12

BEHIND BARS

"Since no verdict had been reached by the jury I lay quietly thinking back on my unfortunate past. After I was well enough to leave the Marine hospital I was taken to a small town which was nearest to the place where I killed those men. Then I was put in jail to await my trial. My fever spells recurred of course but one of the doctors in town was handling my case and kept me feeling pretty good most of the time. While in jail I tried to be a good prisoner. I figured I had done enough wrong. The Jailer and the rest of the prisoners treated me well, so I didn't have any trouble getting along with them. They told me I was too quiet and kind-hearted to be a killer, but the facts proved them wrong. When my problems got too much for me I became a killer, just like all the rest. Soon after they locked me up I began to get lonesome again. I needed someone to talk to so I wrote Brother Ainsworth. I told him about my troubles and explained my need of a friend. I remembered he told me to contact him if I ever needed him, and I surely needed a friend now. I didn't know whether he would respond to my letter or not. If he hadn't I wouldn't have blamed him much. I guess no one wants to deal with a murderer. But he had a *double* reason not to write me. I had no right to ask for his friendship and help after the way I treated his advice in Centerville. But I was all wrong. A letter came from him by return mail. This started a long series of letters back and forth. His friendship was a great strengthening power to me. He tried to see my side of the whole mess and he encouraged me to go ahead and make something out of myself. Others had condemned me. I didn't know how I could do much in jail but at least I was willing to try. Now I was willing to do anything the preacher said."

"Sometime after I had been writing Brother Ainsworth some of the men in the cell next to mine told me I could never be forgiven for my wrongs. They tried to tell me that murder was the unpardonable sin. I didn't know whether this was right or not, so the idea began to worry me. I wrote the preacher immediately and asked him if I could be forgiven and if I could ever have peace of mind in this life again. And in about three days I got my reply. Brother Ainsworth explained that killing could become *an* unpardonable sin, if I didn't repent of it and pray God for forgiveness. But he also told me that the same was true of all other types of sin. Then he mentioned the Apostle Paul's case. He was a murderer too! Yet, he got forgiveness. He said 'And I thank Christ Jesus our Lord, who hath enabled me, for that he counted me faithful, putting me into the ministry; who was before a blasphemer, and a persecutor, and injurious: but I obtained mercy, because I did it ignorantly in unbelief. And the grace of our Lord was exceeding abundant with faith and love which is in Christ Jesus.' This passage comforted me. If Paul could get forgiveness for murder then maybe I could too."

"The preacher then explained that the unpardonable sin was a condition of heart. It couldn't be forgiven because the person was so far gone that he didn't want to return to God's righteousness. Then I began to understand. It wasn't that God wanted anyone to be lost, but that the person had gotten so far into sin that he wouldn't return to God to ask for help. I could see why that would be the unpardonable sin. And when I realized that God would accept anyone back who was truly sorry for his wrongs I was relieved. I had been afraid that God wouldn't forgive me no matter what I did. This gave me a new outlook on God and the Bible. I saw God as the loving Father who wanted no one to perish, 'but that all should come to repentance.' This made the whole question clear to me. If any man is eternally lost it is because he will not turn back to God, and not that God wouldn't receive him back."

"Also in the preacher's letter was the mention of the case of Simon of Samaria. This man became a Christian just like I did, but he too made some mistakes afterwards. The Apostle Peter rebuked him pretty hard for straying, but he didn't say he

156

couldn't be forgiven. As a matter of fact he said the very opposite. He told this erring Christian to 'repent therefore of this thy wickedness, and pray God, if perhaps the thought of thine heart may be forgiven thee.' And the eighth chapter of Acts said the sinner asked Peter to pray on his behalf. That meant that, as a Christian, I would have to repent and pray God's forgiveness. I wrote Brother Ainsworth my thanks for this information and begged him to pray for me as Peter had for Simon. And with the knowledge that someone was praying for me, I came to know peace and contentment of heart. This led me to trust in God as I had never known a human being could."

The Jailer was much impressed with Roger's conduct. He was a model prisoner and never spoke a harsh word to anyone. Instead he encouraged other inmates to try to get along and cause as little trouble as possible. And though he was confined to a jail in a small town he didn't feel that he was completely helpless to improve the world around him. Because of this unselfish attitude Roger began to grow spiritually. His confinement, instead of proving a boring experience to him, became a blessing to him. He was cut off from the busy and competitive world so he had plenty of time to think and to figure out things.

"My interest in the Bible was greatly increased one day when I received a brand new copy as a gift from the Young People's class at the Centerville church. Of course everyone in Centerville knew about my troubles and they were very kind to try to cheer me up. In my new Bible were many kinds of helps which could assist me in finding what I wanted to study. It had a concordance, a dictionary and a general index as well. I could usually find anything I wanted sooner or later in one of these."

Roger's understanding and appreciation of the true moral virtues broadened as he read the books of Psalms and Proverbs. He found them very interesting and he learned a lot of new and practical lessons there.

"Among other things I found out was that a good name is worth more than pure gold. How well I knew that now. And I also read that goodness and kindness are much more to be sought than social rank or worldly riches. The world has that one upside down. Everybody's so busy trying to make money or be somebody that they don't think about the true values in life. But I'm one to be talking. I made the same mistake. Then on further over I read that if a child is trained up right while he is young he will return to that good training sooner or later. And I guess that's right too. Everything Grandma and Grandpa Horton taught me makes sense now. I wonder sometimes why I didn't pay more attention to them when I could have really benefited from their advice. But its no use crying over spilled milk. Then when I studied my New Testament section of the Bible I learned that the first four books are all about the life of Christ and that they were written that the sinner may believe that Christ is God's only begotten Son, and that by believing the sinner might gain everlasting life. Then the book of Acts told me about the beginning of the church and how the first Christians became members. When they were told to 'repent and be baptized . . . for the remission of their sins' they were hearing the first gospel sermon of all times. I was glad that 3,000 of those Jews saw the light and obeyed the gospel. I know how they felt. They were murderers too. Then on through the New Testament I found that the rest of the books were called the Pauline Epistles and told Christians and whole churches how to please Christ. The General Epistles, written by James and Peter and John and Jude were next to last. And last I studied the book of Revelation, written by the Apostle John. It told how the church would be attacked many times through the ages and finally, through the help of Christ, win over the Devil's forces. The part that comforted me most was that verse in the second chapter. It said 'be thou faithful unto death and I will give thee a crown of life.' That was what I wanted now. I didn't think anyone would try to kill me because I was a Christian, but I was afraid that I might not remain faithful to God through my trials ahead."

Sometime after Roger's confinement Brother Ainsworth wrote him, asking him about the time of his coming trial. Roger's reply read:

"Dear Brother Ainsworth,

"Yes I have my Bible with me at all times and read it every day. I also pray for forgiveness every day several times. I know it will take a lot of praying if my worthless soul is spared.

"No, I can truthfully say that I never intended to do what I have done. I have never plotted a crime of any kind.

"However, I feel that I have found grace in the Lord. I don't worry about the outcome of my trial any longer. Whatever they decide to do to me is only the judgment of the earth. My concern now is the great reckoning after awhile. And right now I feel that I am better off than some of those who will decide my fate. At least I've found God through my dreadful experience. And I doubt if some of them ever will. If they could just realize that their indifference toward God and religion is a far greater crime than mine, I feel that they would all rush to their Bible for guidance to the better life."

"My time was getting short and the preacher could sense it through the serious nature of my letters. He kept asking me important questions to see if I understood what the scriptures taught about Heaven and the Great Judgment. He knew I was looking at life gravely now and he wanted to help me keep my thoughts and attitudes Christian. There was a possibility at least that I might soon pass on into the boundless eternity where time is not reckoned, and he wanted me to be fully prepared for the trip."

One of the big reasons the preacher kept asking Roger so many questions was that he wanted to find out where the homes and churches, as well as the communities in America, were falling down in the guidance of their young people. Brother Ainsworth had always considered Roger a problem-child to some extent, but never did he think that his young friend would end up a murderer. The preacher asked himself again and again "where did we let Roger down?" Then he dismissed the idea. He had done all he could and the elders had done all they could, but Roger hadn't listened to them at all. He went his own way regardless of the counsel of others.

"One day Brother Ainsworth asked me to state the primary cause of my crime, as I saw it. I wrote him back the only reason I could think of now."

"Dear Brother Ainsworth,

"I know that I should have studied my Bible more and lived closer to Christ. But I used to think I was too busy. I had parties and dances to go to. I was sure a shallow thinker then wasn't I? And even after I got interested in the activities at the church I met Margie and quit nearly all of them. I remember when I even wished I didn't have to go to the regular services any more. I wanted that time to be with Margie too. Then after I left Centerville I quit going to church like I should and just lost out. I got farther away all the time and it seemed that I could never get back.

"Margie and I talked once about how we would start studying our Bible together after our marriage, but we never did. We thought we were too busy. And too, Margie didn't think church people had any fun. I tried to convince her that we had lots of fun at our class parties but since she had never gone to any of them she didn't believe it. She was pleasure-happy and I got that way too.

"I shudder to think of how many young people today are making the same mistakes we did. If they could only understand that terrible rewards come from walking in the paths of this pleasure-seeking world, they wouldn't persist in them. Their problems are very close to my heart now. I guess I feel like that rich man in the sixteenth chapter of Luke. After he died and went to hades he wanted Lazarus to go back to earth and warn his five brothers about the flames there. Well, I know the hades of being a murderer and I know what put me here too. I think I can tell young folks what's bad for them and they'll listen to me. I've had experience, I'm sorry to say.

"There's a favor I want to ask of you. I want you to tell all the young people you can about my failures in life. Tell them in your classes how I had every opportunity to be a good Christian, but I acted foolishly. I chose the world and its sins to God and His righteousness. And I ended up not having any fun after all. I regret most of my past life very much. It could have been so different.

"Then there's another thing I've had on my mind. I've been thinking a lot about death. Now I know its only the separation of the soul from the body, but when that takes place the person doesn't live here any more does he? I used to always think that death was for old folks, but I'm changing my mind about that. Everyday I read about more and more highway wrecks in which young people are killed. That's just speed and carelessness. Those kids are dying before their time. I don't see any reason for it! But I don't see any reason for young people dying through other causes either. Take those in my shape for instance. I'm not thirty years old yet, but I may die pretty soon. It's funny, I had always connected death with age. I didn't pay much attention when a person around eighty years old died. I figured it was their time. But sixteen and seventeen-year old kids! it just doesn't seem right. Youth and death don't mix. They're not supposed to. But they *are* these days. There's nothing we can do about people growing old, I know, but MUST THE YOUNG DIE TOO?"

Brother Ainsworth paused a long time after reading Roger's last question. Must the young die too? They were doing it, but was it necessary, he wondered? Then he reached a decision. No, they don't have to die because of their youthful foolishness. He believed that they could be brought to reason, if they were

161

approached in the right way. But first their parents and church and civic leaders would have to be aroused to their youthful needs. They would have to be willing to spend a lot of time and money to provide wholesome environments for their young off-spring. And they would have to meet the challenge of the competitive world of amusement too. More than ever, the Devil has stationed his lures in convenient places and they beckon to young boys and girls to leave home and leave the church and come have fun. But that isn't the whole story. The wages of sin have yet to be paid. No, the preacher was determined that young people should at least have a chance. He would do all in his power to see that they had the right teachings available to them and some examples to guide them in their way.

"It was several weeks later when Brother Ainsworth wrote me and asked if I had heard from my mother or sisters lately. I thought that was strange. I thought he knew my mother had been dead a long time. And as for my sisters, I was hearing from them regularly now and their pledges of loyalty to me were comforting. But I had heard nothing from Margie or Billy. In my next letter I admitted to the preacher that he had been right about her."

"Dear Brother Ainsworth,

"You were right about Margie. I see it now. She *has* given me many more hours of suffering than she ever did of happiness. Your prophecy came true in almost every detail. My love was too blind to see it in Center-ville.

"I know now that it was through misunderstanding and my lack of love for God that my footsteps went astray. I wouldn't listen to any criticisms of Margie at all. I wouldn't even admit her faults to myself.

"I've had plenty of time to review my past since coming here and I've looked back many times and tried to figure out where I first got off the right track. I've jotted down some notes on everything that I figure influenced my life.

162

"First, there was my early HOME. It was wonderful for a year or two but when DADDY began to go down we had nothing but misery. He couldn't have loved his family as much as he said he did. If he had he wouldn't have disgraced us that way. That's when I first learned to distrust men. And those lumber-jacks smelled just like daddy the night I rode with them. I didn't trust them from the first.

"Then, there were my GRANDPARENTS who became my guardians. They didn't ruin my philosophy of life or anything like that, but they didn't help it much either. Grandpa meant well and did his best I suppose, but I thought his methods were too severe. He made me feel that the world was a hard place. Now I can appreciate what he was trying to do, but I sure didn't understand then. However, if I'd have listened to his good advice I wouldn't be here today.

"My SCHOOLMATES were all good kids, but they didn't give me much milk of human kindness. They never let me feel equal to them, nor did I ever quite feel wanted. I didn't mind their jokes and teasing, but sometimes they hurt my feelings pretty bad. Some of them didn't know when to quit. I hope you can get the kids at home to lay off the unfortunate students at school. Their burden is heavy enough without someone piling it on, like they did me. Take it from me, those kind of young people need help, not kicking around.

"I've had quite a time trying to figure what part the CHURCH played in my life. I know the members did the best they could, and the leaders too as far as that goes, but still there was something lacking. The members never seemed to accept me into their friendship. I even wondered at one time if they liked each other, but now I know they did. They just didn't go out of their way to show it. That's one of the reasons I waited as long as I did to become a Christian. I didn't know whether they wanted orphans in the church there or not. Things

163

were awful dull when I first went there. But later when the teachers began to use flannel boards and sand tables to teach us I got to enjoying my studies more. All those helps were wonderful in making clear to us what people looked like in Christ's day and how they dressed and all. I'm sorry now that I didn't insist on Margie's attending services with me each Sunday. That might have made a big difference in our later life.

"The place I really went wrong was my choice of RECREATION. I don't mean that it was all wrong or anything like that. But I see now that the no-name club was the worse group of kids in town and their influence was only for bad. Our frequent visits to the dances and later to the taverns didn't strengthen my moral fiber. But being with some young people and having a good time was the most important thing in my life those days. I would have defied anyone who tried to change me— and I guess I did. I marvel too how the club pulled me around by the nose. I sure was stupid, wasn't I? I had a mind and will of my own, but I didn't use them. I thought I had a lot of fun there for awhile, but now I know it wasn't worth it. You tried to tell me that the wages of sin is death, but I thought that was a lot of bunk.

"My next mistake was MARGIE. She was plenty bad medicine, but I didn't know it then. I knew she drank and smoked, but that didn't change my mind about her. I wonder if anything could have changed my feelings toward her then? You certainly tried, but I thought you were nosing in my business too much. We really came from two different worlds, Margie and I did. She was from that rough kind in New York and I didn't know any kind of people but the simple kind of folks at Centerville. But she put on a good front. And she led me right into her trap.

"Then there was my NIGHT WORK down at the traffic-control office. Margie was happy until then.

Maybe we were going to make the grade but that ended it. I thought we needed the money more than we needed to be together. But now I know you can't have a happy family unless they can all be together and do things together. Anyway I blundered terrible by refusing to heed Margie's pleas to change jobs. My own stubbornness was the real start of our trouble. I think I killed her love by refusing to try to see her side to things. Maybe that's why she left me the second time.

"But my greatest mistake was FORGETTING GOD. I was stronger than Margie about spiritual matters. I had had more opportunities to know what to do, but I let them slip. If we had trusted God to help us settle our differences, then both of us would have given in at the first and our marriage would still be strong. I take the blame here. I should have known better.

"Many of my friends have tried to convince me that I was only a victim of circumstances and there is no doubt in my mind that this played a leading role, but that's not all the story. My misfortunes were a lot my own making. I had many advantages, but I would listen to no one. I was Big Chief Roger and no one could tell me anything! And think of this too; there were a lot of kids who were worse off than I but they made good lives for themselves. No, I'm afraid I chose the kind of life I wanted and I'm only reaping what I sowed.

"Besides writing letters I spent a lot of my time in jail reasoning with other prisoners. I tried to get them interested in religion, but most of them wouldn't listen to me. Most of them made fun of me for even talking about it. But that didn't stop me for one minute. I just talked to somebody else. Time was fleeting for me so I tried to use it to the best advantage. It hurt me though to see how blind those men were. They were as blind as I had been a few years before. They couldn't get this world and its cheap riches out of their way so they could see the real riches of life."

All of Roger's efforts didn't go to waste however. Once in a great while a man would listen to him. In all, three men learned the truth due to his patience with them. The local minister of the Lord's church came over and got permission to take them to the church building to be baptized for the remission of their sins. All three of them were in for short terms and each promised to make a new life for himself on the outside.

"This success as a Bible instructor thrilled me beyond words. Now I could say my life hadn't been entirely in vain. I was bubbling over when I shared my success with the preacher."

"Dear Brother Ainsworth,

"I am very happy in my study of the Lord's Word and in teaching it to others here. The sermon books you sent me are increasing my knowledge of the truth a great deal. Thanks very much for them. Bible teaching is badly needed by these men. Most of them have never studied the Bible for themselves. Very few of them have ever attended church services much either. But the strange thing about it is that I have yet to find one of them who deliberately planned to end up in here. Most of them just got careless like I did and went too far.

"My trial comes up pretty soon they tell me, but I no longer fear, for should I walk through the valley of the shadow of death the Lord will be with me."

CHAPTER 13

AN UNEXPECTED VISITOR

THE AMBER AND RED autumn leaves had now turned to a deep
brown outside Roger's jail window. They had turned loose their
hold on the tree branches and had been wrestled to the ground
by the wintry breezes. The trees stood naked against the horizon
of low gray clouds and their slender fingers pointed up toward
the rain and sleet which was threatening to come down.

"The picture outside my window was painted in hues of
gray, brown and black. It brought gloom and dispair to my
heart. The shadows at night seemed to represent death and the
heart-rending melancholy that accompanies it. Summer and Fall
had been beautiful and Spring had been gay. But now the green
grass and leaves were brown or a dirty black. All that remained
of life were the evergreens and perennial bushes. It was a
struggle for me to stay cheerful through these winter months,
however, the days passed by rapidly because each new dawn
brought me closer to my trial."

"Most of my time now was spent in reading my Bible. Every
day I picked up a few new nuggets of golden truth and I made
notes of them and then stored them away among my other
treasures. But one Sunday morning my Bible reading was interrupted. The Jailer told me I was wanted in the office. I
didn't pay this much mind. I got special privileges every once in
awhile. Sometimes it would be a gift from someone in town or
a special package. And occasionally I got to sample one of the
Jailer's wife's fresh cakes. I tried to be the best prisoner I knew
how so they weren't afraid I'd try to run away."

"But this time it was different. It was a treat alright, but a
better one than I had enjoyed in years. The Jailer's wife met me
at the door and showed me to a chair. On the other side of the

room was another lady. I didn't know her. She was middle-aged and was dressed real fancy and smiled at me a lot. At first I thought she favored someone I knew, but then I figured it was just my imagination. Then the Jailer's wife, Mrs. Wrie introduced us."

"Now you make yourself comfortable over there Roger, and get perfectly at ease. We've got a wonderful surprise for you. I want you to meet Mrs. Olsen here. Mrs. Olsen, this is Roger."

"I could tell that a lot of the formality was Mrs. Wrie just putting on. Underneath her smile was almost a smirk and I began to sense that she was concealing something from me."

"Dad and me will be here in the other room Roger, you just call us if you need us. Now we're going to let you and Mrs. Olsen get better acquainted."

"This was all very peculiar behavior, I thought. I didn't understand why they would leave me in the office with a complete stranger. But then I understood better after a few minutes."

"Roger, I know this is all very strange to you, but I asked for it this way. There is something I want you to know and I wanted to tell you myself. Its really very awkward. But first, tell me, do you recognize me?"

"By now I was getting mighty suspicious. Her eyes did look familiar and the way she smiled reminded me of my sisters. The thought flashed through my mind that that was one of my aunts. I told her she looked familiar, but I couldn't recognize her. It was then that she broke down and told me."

"Roger, darling! I'm . . . I'm your mother! Don't you remember me?"

"Mother's last words were spoken so softly I nearly missed them. Then I tried to register what she had just said. She told me she was my mother, but my mother was dead—had been since I was a little boy. But she did look very familiar. I was skeptical at first and I drew back and looked at her strangely. This was quite a blow to me."

"Roger, Roger I'm your mother. I just heard about your trouble and came as fast as I could."

"I was not convinced yet. It's hard to accept something all of a sudden that you've disbelieved for years. And mother had changed so much from the picture I had of her. She was gray-haired now and her face was full of wrinkles. And her eyes were a dull blue where they had been a deep and beautiful blue when I was a kid. I wanted to believe her, but it didn't seem possible."

"I know this has all been a horrible nightmare for you, son, but I'm here now and I'll stay by your side from now on. Roger, you still look at me as though you don't believe me! Mom and Dad Horton are in the other room and they can prove I'm your mother. Oh, please believe me! Don't look at me that way. I'm your mother and I want you to love me."

"I glanced at the door and Grandpa Horton smiled and nodded to me. Then I believed. I had wanted to believe all the time but something kept holding me back. It didn't seem real and this news came as such a shock."

When tears began to flow from Roger's eyes his mother rushed to him and embraced him as she showered him with kisses.

"Honey, I've been a terrible mother to you. I deserted you and you're in trouble now. Oh, sweetheart can you ever forgive your mother? Can you ever forgive her?"

"Mother was trembling so that she could hardly talk, but that didn't matter to me now. It was the most wonderful experience of my life to hold her in my arms. For thousands of nights I had dreamed about her. I even tried to pattern my whole life after all the good qualities I had remembered in her. But this was more wonderful than all my dreams and it was the fulfillment of my fondest hope. Just knowing that I had a mother after all changed a lot of things after this."

Roger and his mother clung to each other for a long time and spoke comforting words. Each was concerned about the other's welfare and wanted to know so many things.

"Finally mother and I sat down on the couch and talked and talked and talked. She told me about meeting Mr. Olsen in the city and marrying him and neglecting the children. She admitted that she lost her mental balance and craved security and a home and was afraid to tell her new husband. He didn't like children."

"Mother, that's all in the past now. It's all over. We're together again and that's all that matters. This is the happiest day of my life! This is wonderful!"

"But Roger, can you forgive mother? I know I don't deserve it, but I'll die if you don't forgive me. I couldn't stand it."

"Now, now, mother. Don't cry any more. What's happened is in the past. It's all over. There's nothing we can do about that. Now all we can do is hope and pray for forgiveness. I've found peace with God and that's my greatest comfort now. You can find rest with Him too. All you have to do is ask Him. We can still be happy no matter what happens. If we know God then we can understand a lot of things other folks can't. Believe me, I know what I'm saying. I've done a lot of wrong things in the past few years, but I'm free from them. The Lord's forgiven me. I feel sure of it."

It was after dark when Roger and his mother finished talking. When they were through the Hortons came in and the four of them enjoyed a brief family reunion.

"Closing time came much too soon for me that evening. Mother and the Hortons had to leave but they promised to be back the next day. And they left me happy beyond words. I had a mother after all. Those kids had been wrong about me being an orphan— I had a mother *too*. I guess I was childish about it, but finding out I had a mother—after so long—was such a thrill to me. I felt warm all over and my heart was aglow. When I got back to my cell I couldn't hold the good news so I told all the men about my good fortune. Most of them were happy with me, but some scoffed. But that didn't dampen my spirits. I had too much good fortune to be discouraged by anything. Then after we quieted down I got on my knees to share my joy with the Lord. I knew He was interested. I had read that He was as concerned about our happiness as He was our sorrows. I don't know how long I prayed or how many times I said the same thing over, but I must have thanked Him a hundred times for letting me see my mother again. The next morning I awoke much earlier than usual. I was still overflowing with joy and I had to share it with some- one, so I wrote Brother Ainsworth about it. I guess that was the happiest letter he'd ever received. He answered me in a few days and asked me what I knew about my trial. He said he hoped to be present if his schedule worked out. I wrote him back about the date of my trial."

"Dear Brother Ainsworth,

"My trial has been postponed for awhile, so I don't know just when it will be. However, I am still in high spirits. Now I have my mother and the Hortons and you to stand beside me. And I know God will be with me too. I've asked Him to be there many times. As to my feelings? They can't hurt me now for my earthly feelings left me some time ago. I live only in the comfort of my Bible and my prayers, as well as letters from friends. Mother's appearance has certainly helped out my morale.

"In your letter you spoke of my not being resentful after all I've been through. It's hard to explain to others, but being a preacher I believe you'll understand. You're accustomed to deep spiritual thoughts. I feel that I have been richly blessed through my sad experiences, rather than abused. As for resentment, families of the men I killed are the ones who feel that. They hate me and have written that they hope I get the limit. But I can't blame them. I've made them suffer so much. They're doing all they can to see that I get the death penalty, but I still don't feel hard toward them. If they were Christians they'd see things different too.

"You know, I've lived a rather full life for my short years and I've seen a lot of things the average person wouldn't see in three life-times. I had a few years of happy home life and I had a good son to make me proud. I enjoyed good wages on my job and had a nice little nest-egg in the bank until Margie took it out. But then I doubt that I would have ever turned to God if our home had remained the same. It took quite a jolt to wake me up, didn't it? But it finally succeeded. And I've seen a lot of folks just like me. They had to get into serious trouble before they turned to the Lord for help. It's a pity we waited too late isn't it? So you see I don't feel too mistreated after all. Through my troubles I've learned what the realities of life are. And without suffering I might never have learned the fear of the Lord and humility. But in spite of my sins, I believe that I will live forever with God. I've done everything you said the Bible required of me, so everything should be right between me and Him now."

Brother Ainsworth marveled at the fine attitude Roger was showing. He couldn't help but think back to Roger's adolescent days when he was so stubborn and headstrong. The preacher wondered if firmer treatment might have straightened his young friend out, but then he doubted it. He tried everything but manhandling him as it was. He remembered that Roger had listened to no one. In his reply to his young friend he asked about his confinement and how he was taking it. The reply pleased him greatly.

"Dear Brother Ainsworth,

"I was just sitting here thinking about my condition when your letter arrived asking about my feelings concerning the outside world. It had dawned on me that I am not missing those things at all. As a matter of fact I don't think they amount to very much. Everybody's out there fighting and scrapping to get more money so they can spend it on more worthless things. And the pity of it all is that those things they buy will all rot and wear out. Then what will they have?

"Here I am in jail, but I'm richer than those people. I have faith in God now, and peace of mind. That's a lot more than most of them have. Things I used to think I had to have to be happy mean nothing to me now. It's funny how values change isn't it? But if folks would take more time to sit down and think out what is really worthwhile they'd change their actions fast. I was out there as busy as could be once myself trying to make more money. I think now that it was greediness that took away my home and spoiled my life.

"No, I don't begrudge the world because of its freedom. I'm grateful to God that I'm permitted to exchange my worldly life of sin for my present life of peace and rest. And above all I'm thankful for the freedom of soul that the love of God has brought me.

"I'm really not much of a writer and certainly no poet at all, but I've tried to put my present feelings into a poem. I've entitled it, *My Trust.*

"Yes, though the road be rough and rugged
    And the hills in my life hard to climb;
I shall lean on the love of Jesus:
    It is here for all mankind.

"And if from the trail I wander,
    I shall ask on bended knee
For God's wonderful help and comfort
    From a place where no eye can see.

"No matter where I wander,
    No matter what others say,
I shall always trust in my Savior,
    And will trust Him all the way.

"Then when the Death Angel calls me,
    And I sink in life's stormy sea,
I know then I shall see Jesus:
    He'll be there to comfort me."

Chapter 14

DEAR BILLY

"The jury was still debating my case. I could hear noises from their room, but none of the raised voices that I had heard hours earlier. While I was waiting for their verdict I went back to the window and looked out. It was the wee hours of the morning and everything was very quiet and still. While I was standing there I began to think what I would do if I were on that jury. How would I vote if I heard the same evidence against someone else that had been brought up against me. Then I admitted to myself that it looked bad. It looked very bad. Murder, theft, AWOL from the Marines; it didn't make a pretty picture."

"But what would I say if someone were in my place and I had their fate in my hands? Guilty? Innocent? Would I hold out for life imprisonment? Some of those men in there were probably doing that for me. Would I give a murderer and a thief the chair? Could I? I wondered to myself, could I judge another man without knowing *all* about him? Would I be fair if I did? I concluded my thought with the realization that I couldn't answer that question. Then I began to realize what a task those twelve men in that jury room had before them."

"I got a fair hearing in court—that is on the facts. But when my lawyers tried to review my past life and the many circumstances leading up to my crime, the other side objected. They said my side was trying to prejudice the jury by appealing to their emotions. And the Judge upheld their charge. We never got to tell them about all the times others had mistreated me. They just told how I mistreated others. But I guess that's the way court trials go. I had been warned to expect some smooth maneuvering by the State's attorneys and they lived up to their reputation. Things looked pretty bad for me after the trial was over, but some of those jurymen looked sorta favorably at me as they left the room. Maybe things won't be as bad as I fear."

Roger heard someone in the courtroom so he arose and walked to the door and peered out to see who was coming. Two men were approaching. One was a policeman but he didn't know who the other one was.

"O. K. mister, you can stay about twenty or thirty minutes. When you're through just knock on the door. I'll be outside."

"Howdy Roger, I'm with the NEWSFLASH magazine. My name's Don Williams. I'm from Chicago. The boss sent me down here to get an exclusive from you as well as cover your trial. Things sure looked bad out there last night didn't they? Boy, it wouldn't surprise me if you get a new trial. Most of us news guys thought you should have been free to tell all that stuff, you know, all about the hardluck you had. Man, that would have made juicy reading. You know, human interest. That's the kind of stuff our readers like."

"Well I'm glad to meet you Mr. Williams. I'm not familiar with your magazine, but I bet it's a good one. Now what is it you want from me?"

"Look pal, there hasn't been any other guys around here asking for a story has there?"

"No. None except those who asked for statements after the jury went out. They're the only ones. Why?"

"Why, because I want an exclusive from you. That's why. And if every magazine in the country has something exclusive from you mine won't be very exclusive. See? Now here's what I want you to do. Tell me something about yourself. Something those other guys don't know. Make it something flashy. Something that'll read real good. Know what I mean?"

"No I don't. Maybe you'd better explain what you want."

"Oh, give me something I can glamorize. It don't have to be true. Just start it out true and I'll finish it up the way we want it. You know the truth usually isn't very exciting to readers, so we have to doctor it up a little. You know, stretch things a little."

"Now wait a minute Mr. Williams. I'm not going to tell any lies. I'll be glad to tell you the truth, but that's all. I've tried that

175

lying before and nothing good comes from it."

"O.K., O.K., so you want to do it clean. I don't guess it matters that much. Now here's my offer. I'll give you $200 for some facts about yourself that you haven't told anybody. In other words I'm offering to pay you to tell me something you won't tell anybody else. That clear?"

"Sure that's clear, but what do you want to know?"

"Oh, maybe you could tell me something about your past life. You didn't get to tell that on the stand yesterday and everybody seemed to want to hear all of it. Now is the $200 alright with you?"

"No sir, it isn't. I'd like more than that if I could get it. I've got a good reason for wanting it. What about, say $600."

"Pity my expense account! I haven't got that kind of money. Why my publishers would fall over dead if I sent them a bill that big. But I tell you what I'll do. I'll up it a hundred. Say $300?"

"That's only half enough. I gotta have at least $600. Sure enough, can't you go that high? After all, you're asking me to do you quite a favor."

"I donno, Mack. It all depends on what you want it for. I might go that much, but what you give me would really have to be good."

"I'll tell you what I want it for. If I got $600 for my story you could give $200 each to the Miles, the Peebles and the Southys. Those are the widows of the men I killed. I've wanted to do something for them since they're in pretty hard circumstances with their breadwinners gone. Come on, can't you help me just that much?"

"Say that's pretty white of you, wanting to give the money away. I thought you wanted it for yourself. Yeah, maybe we can work this thing out. One condition though! Give me permission to tell what you're going to use the $600 for. I think the boss'll buy that. As a matter of fact I'm sure he will. Now what can you tell me that hasn't been told before?"

"You got me there. I'm not a newspaper man, so I don't know what people want to know. What do you suggest?"

"Think hard, Mack. There's bound to be something interesting

176

you haven't told about yourself. Were you a high school champ at anything? Or an honor student? Or did you win any kind of honors in college?"

"No, none of those things. I didn't excell at anything in high school and I didn't go to college. Say, you'll split that $600 with those three families won't you?"

"Sure I will, that is if I get something that good. Now think. What hasn't been told about you yet? Don't you think of anything?"

"No sir, I don't. I just can't think of anything, but I want that $600 pretty bad. You try suggesting something."

"Well, look here. You gotta beat this. Think of my deadline! I've got to call something in by five. Say, what about this? You'll admit that your life didn't turn out like you planned it, did it?"

"That's right. I never dreamed I'd be in any kind of trouble like this. I had it all planned different—perfect marriage, ideal home, you know, things like that."

"Great! great! Now you've got something. Let's see. Murderer Misses Goal. No, that's no good as a title. Let me try again. Murderer . . . No I don't like that word. You don't act like a murderer to me, so I'll not use that word. A Killer's Dream. Say, how do you like that? Pretty nice isn't it. That's the title I'll use. Killer doesn't sound as bad as Murderer, does it? Now I'll just sit here and take notes and you spill it. Tell me the dream-life you planned. I'll stop you if I want to know any extra details. Now go ahead."

●

"I'll start with my high school days. Things went along pretty good until then. Well, let's see. I was a junior in high school when I first got off my course, so I'll begin there and tell it straight through just as I had hoped it would come true."

"I was a Christian young man just trying to get along in the world and be a success at whatever I went into. Of course I was getting interested in girls about this time, but I was going to be very careful about who I got. I'd been told that one's marriage could either make or break the person, so I planned to be careful. First of all, I didn't date any girls except those who went to church. Usually they visited services with me some. That may sound old fashioned, but I figured marriage was too big a risk with a girl that didn't like to go to church."

"At first my best girl, Margie didn't want to go to services with me. She was running around with a fast crowd that made the highway taverns at night and all, but I soon got her out of that. I told her to take her choice. Me or the crowd. You see, they had tried to get me in their gang too, but when I found out what they were I quit them. Margie quit them too. I guess we were really in love, for her to do that. I told her I didn't want a smoking, drinking, dancing wife. And I was ready to quit her too. I told her if she had to run with that trashy type she could have them, but not me. I valued my Christian character and influence too much for that. But don't get me wrong! I didn't have any of that 'holier than thou' attitude, I just didn't like the low kind of life, that's all. My grandparents taught me better."

"Instead of making the high school dances, our crowd had their own parties. Those kids' folks were swell. They spent a lot of time and money just entertaining us, but now I see it was worth it. That way none of us missed the wrong recreation. We were having too much clean fun to notice it. Margie bucked about this for awhile too but I stood my ground again. I told her I didn't go in for that questionable entertainment. I thought too much of my reputation in the town and at the church for that. I was leading public prayers by now and filling in for the teacher of my Bible school class and I couldn't do that with a bad reputation."

"Anyway, Margie stuck by me through thick and thin and we got married. Our little wedding wasn't much, but it impressed us a lot. Brother Ainsworth, that's the preacher where I worshipped, said the ceremony. Then after the wedding my grandparents gave us a small reception at their house. We were the happiest kids in town."

"We got a trip to Atlantic City as our wedding present from Granddad. And when I got home I had a job at the Centerville bank waiting for me. Grandpa got that for me. But I almost didn't take it. Margie's father got me a job in New York City, but at the last minute I decided not to take that one. I wasn't a big city boy and was afraid things might get too much for me up there. I could handle my problems in our little city, so I decided to stay home and work. Margie was unhappy about my decision for awhile, but after we bought our little place out on Broadus street and got it fixed up she settled down. I worked in the bank and she got a job at the children's shop for awhile, but she gave that up when Billy came along. That's our son. He's about four or five now. Anyway he was a fine boy. But back to my dream. Then Margie and I worked hard and made a name for ourselves in the town."

"We were getting along just fine until the war came along. Then when World War II broke out I had to go into service for awhile. I sure hated to leave home. We had our place in first class shape and I knew Margie couldn't keep everything up, but that was part of the price of war I guess. I also had a promotion coming at the bank, but I didn't get it before I left. When my draft call came I went ahead to get it over with. The folks at the church gave me a little pocket-sized New Testament as a going away present and Margie gave me a new Bible to do my heavier studying in. Both of them got a lot of use before I got home again and I appreciated them very much."

"When I got to the induction center I found that the services were low on men and the restrictions were eased up for awhile. I chose the Marine Corps. and got my boot camp training at Paris Island."

"That Paris Island, South Carolina?" the reporter interrupted.

"That's right, and from there I went to Diego and shipped out. I was a guard on the USS Marlborough. On the way over to Pearl Harbor I went down with undulant fever. Had a bad case too for awhile. But they fixed me up at the Naval hospital there and I was ready to go again. I didn't go on with my group though because they went into the battle zone weeks before. Finally they shipped me back to the States and I spent the rest of my time in the Marine offices in California."

"V-E Day and V-J Day finally came and a lot of the soldiers got their discharges. The boys who had been over in those jungles got home first. But I didn't mind staying in a year longer. Margie and Billy were there with me a lot of the time so I was happy. Then when I got my discharge I went back to the bank at Centerville and got my job back and the promotion to boot. They said my experience in the Marine offices made me a more valuable man. After that I worked hard, and I studied banking a lot too. The directors told me I had the making of a bank official if I would continue to apply myself. Of course that sounded good to me and I did try hard."

"And to make a long story short, I had always dreamed of being the bank president some day. Then when I walked around the town the people would smile at me and show me respect. Too, I hoped to one day be an elder in the church, like my grandfather. Those two things. No, three. I wanted to be a successful business man, a good Christian and a good husband and father. That's the kind of life I always prayed for. Its one of those they-lived-happily-ever-after kind of stories isn't it?"

●

"Yeah, guess it is kid. But tell me something. If that's the kind of a life you always dreamed of having, how come you to end up in this hoosegow? There's quite a difference in this story you've just told me and the one they told yesterday in your trial."

"The difference, Mr. Williams is in knowing to do right, but not doing it. I could have had my dream-life. My grandparents and friends and my preacher friend did everything they knew to do. But I didn't listen to them. It was just a case of not listening to good advice I guess."

Just as the reporter turned another page in his notebook the bailiff knocked on the door. The jury was returning and everyone was being summoned into the courtroom for the reading of the verdict. Roger shook hands with the feature-writer and walked out in the courtroom to his seat. The room was practically empty at this early hour of the morning. Roger's mother and sisters were there and a few friends. Brother Ainsworth was called away during the night by the death of one of the elders of the church in Centerville, so he did not hear the reading of the jury's decision.

"The jury was already seated when I got to my place. They were a tired-looking group of men. Some of them had red eyes and I could tell they had been crying. All of them looked very solemn. Then the Judge came in. He was sleepy-eyed and tired too. Finally, he got everyone quiet in the room and asked for the verdict of the jury."

"Will the foreman of the jury step forward please. Mr. foreman, have you gentlemen reached a verdict?"

"We have, your honor. We find . . . . . we find the defendant guilty as charged!"

The audience gasped and Roger's mother and sisters broke into unrestrained sobbing. The Judge waited patiently until order was restored a few minutes later.

"Then, according to the laws of this State, it is my solemn obligation to pronounce sentence."

"The bailiff came over to me and asked me to rise. Then he ushered me up before the Judge.

"Roger Scott, you have been found guilty of first-degree murder. The sentence of this court is that you shall die in the electric chair for your crimes."

The news of Roger's crime and imprisonment had escaped Margie's and Ben's attention because they lived so far away from the place where it all happened. But after his conviction and sentencing to death it would have been hard for them to miss it. United Press, Associated Press and International News Service wires all carried the story to the nation. And in addition to the newspaper stories were the radio reports.

The little weekly newspaper at Orango, Florida also carried the story the following Friday. Other citizens in Orango paid the news little mind. To them it was another case of a criminal getting his just deserts.

But with Margie and Ben it was different. When she read the account of Roger's trial and the outcome she screamed without realizing what she was doing. Terror seized her heart. This was the first news she had received of Roger since their divorce. She and Ben had moved as far away from him as they could, hoping that he would never find them. They were even living under assumed names and had told everyone in town that Billy was their child.

When Margie finished reading the article she rushed into the bedroom and thrust the paper into Ben's hands. She was in hysterics.

"Look Ben, that's about Roger. He's in trouble. What are we going to do? They're going to kill him! What can we do about it?"

Ben cursed violently and threw the paper on the bed. Then he began to pace back and forth across the room.

"What are we going to do? What do you mean, what are we going to do? We're not going to do anything. We're just going to keep our mouths shut. You see, I was right! I told you we wouldn't get away with it. You and your bright ideas! I don't know what you're going to do, but I'm going to get out of here. I've had enough."

After the sentence was read Roger was returned to the small-town jail for further confinement. His first act was to write Brother Ainsworth.

"Dear Brother Ainsworth,

"My trial is at long last finished and they found me guilty. I'm sorry you had to leave before the Judge sentenced me. I was counting on you standing with me before the Judge. And mother needed you too. She and Maree and Jan and Sue took the verdict awfully hard. I think mother nearly fainted.

"Of course the verdict of guilty means death. However, I'm still in good spirits for I know God has forgiven me, even though those men could not.

"I am enclosing the names and addresses of my sisters. I want you to write them and explain to them the peace that I have gained through a closer walk with God. You know how to say these things far better than I do. Maree is taking my sentence the hardest so please write her first. She will need to understand the rightness of it all. Your explanation of my inward peace will ease her pain some. I feel selfish in asking this much of your time, but you can put my thoughts into words so well."

The case of the State verses Roger Scott was appealed to the State Supreme Court on grounds that all testimony in favor of the defendant was not allowed to be presented. This caused another long delay in the case until Roger could be given another trial or the date of his execution could be set. His lawyers prepared a brief in which they charged that he was physically and mentally ill at the time of his crime and therefore was not morally accountable. They contended that the jury did not get to hear the facts which would have supported this view.

Roger settled back into the routine jail life while he waited the outcome of his appeal.

"I read my Bible now as I had never read it before and I prayed a lot too. My destiny would be decided finally by the high court and I hoped and prayed that they would give me another chance. My only comfort now were my many friends and their letters. To Brother Ainsworth I wrote:

'Dear Brother Ainsworth,

'No one knows how long or how short my time on earth will be now. Only God knows that. But if it is His will that my sentence on earth should be carried out, then I shall go my way smiling. I will have been judged on earth for my sins and will have been punished for them. Then I feel that God will no longer hold them against me. I have done all I know to do to make matters right between us. My only request now is that God will be with me during my moments of weakness and bear me up. I am no longer afraid to die for the Lord is my light and my salvation. To Him I will commit my soul.'"

"A week went by and then a month and still we heard nothing from the Supreme Court. The wait was a long one for me and a trying period in my life. But I held up thanks to my many prayers for help. And the letters I received helped cheer me up also."

Most of Roger's letters were from close friends or curious people who had read about his trial in the newspapers or magazines. And in time he became familiar with all the handwritings on the envelopes. But one Friday he received a letter with a most familiar handwriting. At first he was afraid to open it. He was afraid that it couldn't be true. The handwriting was Margie's.

"My dearest Roger,

"I have just read about your terrible trial and the death penalty they have given you. I had no idea you were in trouble. I didn't think things would turn out this way, honest I didn't.

"Ben and I have both been out of our minds. We feel that we are to blame for this. If you go to that electric chair we'll always feel that we sent you there. We will have murdered you! But I feel the blame most. It was my idea that Ben and I marry. I was lonesome without you and couldn't stand staying in Westvalley. I picked up the first man that came along and told him a bunch of lies and got him to marry me. I got the divorce on a bunch of lies too.

"Roger, your pleading letters have haunted me day and night for months. You tried to save our marriage and our home, but I went crazy. A lot of other girls did the same thing. They left their husbands too. Oh, Roger if you die, I'll die with you. I can't stand to think of what I've done to you. Can you ever forgive me? I've been mean and cruel and selfish! Can I be forgiven?

"Ben doesn't know I'm writing you. He'd kill me if he did, so he mustn't find out. I think he's gone mad. At times I think he's going to kill me and Billy both, so please don't tell anyone I've written you. But I couldn't let you die without begging your forgiveness.

"Billy is here beside me. I haven't told him why I'm crying, I just can't bear to. The picture enclosed was made of him about a week ago. You'll find that he's growing to be a fine young man. He looks a lot like you.

"Oh Roger, I'm terrified. There's no telling what Ben may eventually do. I'd try to get away from him, but I'm afraid he'd catch us.

"If you care to write me be sure to use the name and address at the bottom of my letter. This is my next door neighbor and she'll see that I get the letter without Ben knowing it.

"Please Roger, please forgive me for all I've done. I didn't realize it would come to this. I'm going to try to see you soon and I'll bring Billy. I pray it won't be too late.

With all my love,

Margie"

"When I finished reading Margie's letter my face and shirt were both wet with tears. There was both joy and pity in my heart. At last she had come to her senses and that made me very happy. And Billy was alright too. It was good to hear that. And forgive her? There was no doubt about my forgiving her. She was a sinner just like me and we both needed forgiveness from God. But neither of us could have His forgiveness unless we forgave each other. Sure, I forgave her. I forgave her before she asked."

Roger wrote the new turn of events to the preacher. He also asked his friend to do him a great favor.

"Dear Brother Ainsworth,

"Just one more favor please. And this is a big one. I heard from Margie today. She and Billy are at Orango, Florida. They're not safe there, so will you call the sheriff at Orango and ask him to get them away from Ben and protect them till you and Grandpa Horton can get her? Hurry as fast as you can because we don't know how much more time I've got here.

"The Supreme Court refused to grant me a new trial and I understand the sentence will be carried out without delay. This was what I expected, however, for the men of this world cannot be as understanding and forgiving as God. I expect to hear in a few hours when I am to die. But don't let this trouble you for I am still happy because I believe there is a better life beyond this one. Where then is there cause for me to fear? Death must come to us all sometime."

"Before my letter reached Brother Ainsworth I got another note from Margie. Ben had run off and taken all their money. Margie was so frightened that she was helpless. She was afraid Ben might return one night in his drunkenness and kill them both. She was there alone with Billy and had no means of protection. This news frightened me so I persuaded the Jailer to let me call Brother Ainsworth long distance. He took the information and agreed to call the sheriff at Orango and also to start after Margie and Billy as soon as possible."

After the telephone call the Jailer told Roger that the time of his execution had been finally set, but that the lawyers were making one last appeal to the Governor of the State for a 30-day reprieve which was the usual custom. However, the Governor was in Washington and they were having difficulty locating him.

"I went on back to my cell to wait—and pray. I prayed earnestly and fervently for the Lord to hold up my execution until I could hold my wife and my child in my arms once again. Then I would be ready to go. I wanted to ask just

186

one more thing of Margie, that she would promise to rear Billy to be a Christian boy."

As soon as Brother Ainsworth got the telephone message he and Grandpa Horton started the long drive to Margie's. They made record time getting there and as soon as they could get her things they started back to Centerville to pick up Grandma Horton. Then they began their tense drive to the state penitentiary to see Roger.

The group loaded the car at 6:30 and were hurrying madly to see Roger before midnight. But they were delayed at the downtown railroad crossing as the north-bound train unloaded passengers and mail. Then when the train was out of their way they started again. Brother Ainsworth drove as fast as the highway speed limits would allow. Everyone in the car sat strained and fearful. They prayed individually that they would not be too late.

What they did not know, however, was that a final letter from Roger had been dropped on the depot platform in one of the mail bags. Everyone had seen the bag but none suspected that it contained Roger's last words to them. Had they waited a short time longer the station agent would have rushed it to them. Then they would have known that their last efforts were in vain. Roger's letter read:

"My dearly beloved,

"If the State carries out its present plan I shall be dead by the time you read this letter. I shall have departed this earth to be with Christ. Till now the Governor has done nothing toward my appeal and we are afraid they will not find him in Washington in time. However, I am trusting God to do whatever is best for us all.

"I had hoped that I might see you once more before I die. I have prayed God for that last wish, but I was afraid that you could not save Margie and get here in time too. I'm glad you got her away from Ben. She'll be safe from now on.

"And now if God wills that I should suffer this penalty for my misdeeds then I am ready and am humbly grateful that He has seen fit for me to join His beloved flock, for I feel a nearness to Christ.

"And now my precious ones, I bid you all farewell until the day that we shall be together again at Jesus' feet in glory. May God bless us all and preserve our souls for eternity."

It was several hours later when Brother Ainsworth swerved the car into the driveway in front of the State penitentiary. He and Margie and Billy, along with Grandpa and Grandma Horton rushed into the building and met the Jailer's wife coming out. Her eyes were full of tears as she told Margie the sad news. Roger had just died!

The Jailer and his wife had accompanied Roger from their home town for fear that none of his friends would be near him at the last. The local preacher of the Church of Christ had been called and he took Brother Ainsworth's place as Roger said his last prayer. Then Roger arose from his prayer and never opened his eyes again. He was led by the hand to the little execution room and strapped into the chair. When he was asked if he had anything to say he spoke three words, "I forgive all."

When the Jailer came out a few minutes later he had not gained full control of himself. He was led to a couch where he wept bitterly. He had witnessed the death of many men, but this was his hardest experience. Roger had become almost as a son to him. Finally he recovered sufficiently to tell Margie of Roger's last requests. He also had all of his personal belongings. He had planned to send them to Centerville with the body but he gave them to Margie instead. There wasn't much left. Roger left the world poor in goods but rich in faith. There was his old pocket knife, his gold watch and chain, his wedding band Margie had given him at their wedding, his Bible and a bundle of letters. On top of the bundle were two freshly sealed envelopes. One was addressed to

Margie and the other was Roger's letter to Billy. Billy's letter read:

"Dear Billy,

"I have written your mother my last will and testament at the same time I wrote this letter to you. I have asked her not to let you open this until your sixteenth birthday. You should be about a junior in high school—which is a dangerous time in your life. By then your daddy will have been dead a long time. Though he died, as bad criminals do, he was never intentionally bad at heart. He never intended to cause anyone to suffer. But he made a lot of mistakes. He became a killer because he wouldn't listen to others.

"Forgive me, my son, for causing you the shame and disgrace of being the son of an executed murderer. Forgive me for all the pain I have caused you. That was the last thing on earth I ever expected to do.

"Now you are a young man of sixteen. And if you are normal you will think you know a lot, possibly more than the teachers at school or even your mother. But let my experience tell you the truth. You are still young and you need lots of help. You need all the help your mother and Brother Ainsworth and Grandpa Horton can give you. They tried to help me, but I refused to listen. Had I heeded their advice I would be there with you today to guide your boyish feet into the paths of righteousness.

"My birthday presents to you are meager, but they are all I had left of this world. Take the pocket knife. Carry it in your pocket every day as a constant reminder that your dad dreamed one day of taking you hunting and fishing with him. But someone else will have to do that in my place.

"The gold watch and chain are yours too. They are to remind you that time is precious. I lived but twenty-eight years. *Eternity comes too soon.*

"The Bible is yours too. Don't just read it, study it and memorize many of its beautiful passages, especially the 23rd Psalm. That was the last chapter I read before going to meet the Good Shepherd.

"And the ring. I want you to have your bride place it upon your finger at your wedding. It was mine and was given to me by the girl I loved more than life itself. My blessings are upon you and whatever girl you choose as your wife. I only pray that she will be a Christian young lady and that you will make a fine Christian man some day.

"They have just told me that I must make ready to leave this world. I do not fear what is coming. I shall close my eyes in prayer in a moment and I shall never leave the sacred nearness of the One who will guide me through the valley of the shadow of death.

"Be a godly man some day and your daddy's fondest wish shall have come true.

God bless and save us all,

Your daddy"

Ten years later Billy received his birthday presents from his father. He was an active Christian young man and was planning to dedicate his life to the ministry of Christ. He had been led to this decision by the many stories his Christian mother told him about the last years of his father's life on earth. He read the letter amid many tears and as he turned the envelope up to replace the letter a newspaper clipping dropped to the floor.

Roger Scott
Is Given Death

*Hitchhiker Slayer
Will Go to
Electric Chair*

NEWCITY, MARCH 15—(AP) Roger Scott, convicted hitchhiker slayer was sentenced today to death in the electric chair.

The sentence was pronounced early this morning to an almost empty courtroom.

A motion for a new trial was overruled by the judge.

Granted permission to address the court, Scott thanked his attorneys for their defense of him, the jailer for the kind treatment of him and the court for the conduct of the trial.

Scott smiled as he left the courtroom.

Printed in the United States
40988LVS00002B/103-114